HOW TO SHIT IN THE WOODS

An environmentally sound approach to a lost art

Kathleen Meyer

Ten Speed Press

1🅢 Ten Speed Press
Post Office Box 7123
Berkeley, California 94707

First Printing 1989

Cover and text design, and typography by Fifth Street Design
Knees by Brenton Beck
Portrait of Sir Thomas Crapper by Marilla Pivonka
Illustration page viii by Pedro Gonzalez
Chapter opening illustrations by J.S. McVey

Library of Congress Cataloging in Publication Data

Meyer, Kathleen, 1942-
    How to Shit in the Woods.

    1. Mountaineering — Health Aspects — Handbooks,
manuals, etc. 2. Defecation — Handbooks, manuals, etc. I.
Title. RC1220.M6M48   1989   613'.4   89-4995
ISBN 0-89815-319-0

Manufactured in the United States of America

2 3 4 5 – 93 92 91 90 89

Acknowledgements

For Father, who would have approved this subject and in memory of Uncle Ernie, the only other rebel and writer in the family, who delighted and inspired me with his letters for so many years.

A heartfelt thanks goes out to the following people: To Jon Runnestrand who constantly re-affirms my choosing untrodden paths and always reminds me to – above all else, in the face of disaster – keep rowing.

To Mark DuBois and Marty McDonnell who, many years ago now, gently straightened out my ignorant city ways by presenting me with a healthy dose of respect for Mother Nature and offering me the first clues as to what were the real and simple joys in life. And to Mark for his sensitive editing of the manuscript.

To Craig Reisner for further heightening my sensitivities to human impact. To Rick Spittler for hours of environmental brainstorming.

To Howard Backer, M.D., for editing the *giardia* section.

To Bruce and Suzanne Degan, and Michael and Mary Pat Fahey for their encouragement, dinners, and computers. And to Michael for his special and supportive friendship.

To my treasured women friends Carol Newman, Fredi Bloom, Martha Massey, Joanne Solberg, Jennie Shepard, Linda Cunningham, and Jan Reiter for surviving with me through all the nutziness of life's daily turmoil. And to Fredi for her inexhaustible contributions of levity.

To darling Jean Hayes for the blessings of clarity and the freedom to become.

To Edith and Fred Bond, and Ronita and Frank Egger for being my families.

To my mother for believing in me and – at ninety years of age – this subject.

To Silvio Piccinotti for his wonderful old stories, his generous ways, and his invaluable teachings about driving draft horses, which helped keep me grounded and sane through the writing of this manuscript and prepared me for the next evolution in my life.

To Susan Adams for the sweet honesty of her friendship, her unflagging encouragement, and her readings of the manuscript at many stages.

To Suzanne Lipsett, an ace friend and editor, for providing honest but smiling swift kicks.

To Robert Stricker, my agent and dear man, for beating down my door and making everything happen. And to Ten Speed Press for a thoroughly enjoyable publishing process.

And to countless others who offered encouragement, direction, inspiration, instruction, or life-support. To name a few: Connie Thomas, Marilla Pivonka, Bruce Raley, Robert Volpert, Bonnie Evans, Norm Franklin, Art Schemdri, Carolyn Takher, Susan Still, Catherine Fox, Esther Young, Stephen McDade, Lorene and Ron, Cameron Macdonald and John Suttle. And to all those helpful souls – voices without faces – at the Forest Service, the Grand Canyon River Permit Office, the sanitary districts, the San Anselmo public library, and the U.C. Medical Library. And to all at Marin Surplus whom I bugged incessantly.

To, of course, everyone who so unabashedly shared a worst-shit-story knowing that it would be spread before the world. You know who you are; I won't mention any names.

Especially, to Patrick for his love and endless patience.

Contents

I dyde shyte thre grete toordes.

Fables of Aesop, Caxton Translation, Vol. 15, 1484

Introduction

In response to Nature's varied calls, How to Shit in the Woods presents a collection of techniques (stumbled upon by myself, usually in a most graceless fashion) to assist the latest generation of backwoods enthusiasts still fumbling with their drawers. Just as important is the intention to answer a different, more desperate, cry from Nature in conveying essential and explicit environmental precautions about wilderness toiletries applicable to a variety of seasons, climates, and terrains.

For many millennia our ancestors squatted successfully in the woods. You might think it would follow that everybody would know how – by instinct. Nature simply takes its course when a colon is bulging or a bladder bursting. But "its course," I cheerlessly and laboriously discovered, was subject to infinite miserable destinations.

Several seasons of guiding city folks down whitewater rivers both sharpened my squatting skills and assured me I wasn't alone in the klutz department. Frequently, the strife and anxiety experienced in the bushes were greater than any sweat produced by the downstream roar of a monster, raft-eating rapid. Those summers on the river led me to a couple of firm conclusions. *One:* Monster rapids inspire a lot of squatting, which in turn supplies a wealth of study material for *two*. *Two* (and ultimately one of the subjects that prompted this publication): Finesse at shitting in the woods – or anywhere else, for that matter – is not come by instinctively. This might sound as if I were a regular Peeping Joan. But with several dozen bodies behind the few bushes and boulders of a narrow river canyon, I found it practically impossible not to trip over a few – exhibiting all manner of contorted expressions and postures – every day. Generally, a city-bred adult, in dropping his or her pants to squat, can expect to be no more successful in this endeavor than a tottering one-year-old. Shitting in the woods is an acquired rather than innate skill, a skill honed only by practice, a skill all but lost to the bulk of the population along with the art of making soap, carding wool, and skinning buffalo.

We are now several generations potty-trained on indoor plumbing and accustomed to privacy, comfort, and convenience. To a person brought up on the spiffy, silenced, flush toilet hidden away behind the bolted bathroom door, elimination in the backcountry can rapidly degenerate into a frightening physical hazard, an embarrassing mess, or, incredibly, a week-long attack of avoidance-constipation.

Over the last decade, an unprecedented lust for wilderness vacations and exotic treks has exploded out of our metropolitan confines. With the same furor that marked the nineteenth-century race to fulfill Manifest Destiny, rat race victims now seek respite in the wilds from twentieth-century urban madness. Masses of bodies are thundering through the forests, scurrying up mountain peaks, and flailing down rivers, leaving a wake of toilet paper and fecal matter Mother Nature cannot fathom. It's not unrealistic to fear that within a few more years the last remaining pristine places could well exhibit conditions equal to the world's worst slums. Anyone who has come upon a favorite, once-lovely beach or river bank trashed with litter has felt horror at the visual impact. But the veiled environmental impact of the rapidly increasing quantity of human waste in the woods is of even greater concern. Tragically, no longer can we drink from even the most remote, crystal clear streams without the possibility of contracting *giardia*, a disease spread through fecal deposits in or about the waterways – and a disease unknown in the U.S. wilderness prior to the 1970s.

Once the "authorities" have taken over preservation, it is, in my mind, already too late. Rules and regulations imposed by government agencies (though absolutely necessary now in many areas) are themselves rude incursions into majestically primitive surroundings and antipodal to the freedom wildness represents. Rules, signs, application forms, and their ensuing costs are truly a pain in the ass, brought about not solely by increased numbers of people, but also by the innocently unaware and the blatantly irresponsible. The willingness to inspire preservation comes most naturally from those who delight in the wilds; it is they – we – who have the greatest responsibility for respect, care, and education. And it is we who must learn and teach others how and where to shit in the woods.

Author's Note

For several years, *How to Shit in the Woods* lay dormant, a collection of scattered ideas on scraps of lined yellow paper tucked in a drawer, while I grappled with a seemingly insurmountable problem: terminology. How was I to refer to this *stuff* that is pushed and squirted out of the body in response to eating and drinking?

Since the days of Adam men have been announcing that they were going off to take a piss, leak, dump, or crap. Although references to the subject do not abound in history, conjecture would have Eve and her female descendants declaring the same until those allegedly delicate of heart, weak-stomached Victorian ladies began fainting at the sound of such language. Daintiness and propriety contracted an allergy to the foregoing diction, which is considered odious to this day. Yet someday, I suspect, cultural fashion will dictate another sweeping back-to-basics movement and relieve this parlance, currently deemed macho, of its inelegance.

Loathing most things fashionable and having at one time worked with street kids, I confess that my own language can quite easily become delightfully raw and debased. I salute macho (in this instance) in the interest of directness. Still, I was reluctant to begin by offending most readers, education – not alienation – being the goal in mind. The process by which I resolved this semantic difficulty is worth sharing.

In everyday speech around everyday friends, I admit I'm partial to the words *shit* and *pee*. Running through all the alternatives produced no sound solutions. Studding an entire book with *urination, defecation, elimination,* and *stools* seemed depressingly clinical. The seems to emit something foul – I remember them being breathed in whispers. *Bathroom* and *restroom* are euphemisms not applicable in the woods; even *outhouse* and *Porta-Potty* do not fit where they do not exist. *Scats, turds, dung, chips, pellets,* and *pies* are useful mainly in zoology and dirty jokes. *Constitutional* seems overly prissy in addition to being misleading, since I never heard of anything but a "morning" constitutional, easily confused with a brisk turn in the fresh air. *John, johnny, head, potty, wee-wee, pee-pee, whizz, Number One* and *Number Two, tinkle, poop, load, poo-poo, doo-doo, ca-ca,* and "going to see a man about a horse" – all a little indirect or too cutesy.

Next, I tried circumventing the problem by relying on description and avoiding particular terms altogether. But the prose became lengthy and cumbersome; plus, I was certain I'd be accused of not calling a crap a crap. Stuck again, without another noun in sight.

My mind slowly began wandering back over the tangle of verbiage looking for a new trail, something missed. I remembered my father had always purported to be within his genteel rights in using the word *piss* because Shakespeare had employed it. Father's strategy seemed excellent (though he was technically wrong; it was Jonathan Swift), and over the years my refined – verging on priggish – mother did grow, if reluctantly, to accept this argument. Though she never came to use the word herself, in time the wince that wrinkled up her face upon its utterance became barely discernable. Thus, with a solid case in point and mother's brief but significant evolution in mind, a defensible logic began to take hold.

The printed word has a way of inventing truths (as the success of several sleazy national tabloids attests) and of influencing acceptable usage, with *Webster's* dictionary being considered the most reliable reference. A burgeoning excitement seized me as I noted that although my 1957 unabridged edition of *Webster's* contained no mention of *shit*, the library's 1988 edition *did* include the term (aha! 'what do you know?) plus a three line definition – linguistic history in the making.

Next, I remembered something E. B. White wrote about language that, no doubt, had stuck in my mind because of his particular metaphor – rivers being close to my heart:

> *The language is perpetually in flux: It is a living stream, shifting, changing, receiving new strength from a thousand tributaries, losing old forms in the backwaters of time.*

Shit hadn't been lost in any backwater. White might well be horrified by my using his explanation for my justifications, but, unwittingly and to my great joy, I found he supplied more and more defense for my crystalizing rationale:

> *A new word is always up for survival. Many do survive. Others grow stale and disappear. Most are, at least in their infancy, more appropriate to conversation than to composition.*

By no means had *shit* become stale. For hundreds of years *shit* had survived with ease. I knew it to be an old word: I'd seen it as *scitian* in Old English, as *shyte* in Middle English. And currently, *shit* is common in daily conversation. But since Webster's is still proclaiming its usage as "vulgar," I concluded that the word was lolling in its infancy.

With the needed precedent set in 1988, I fell right into keeping with father's old strategy. My lacking the literary stature of a Shakespeare or Jonathan Swift became no matter. Feeling as exuberant as one of E. B. White's thousand burbling tributaries, I proposed to help wash this word, *shit*, downstream to its confluence with greater maturity and on into the ocean of acceptable usage. There it might float around in the company of all other words deemed proper for composition. And so it was that I comfortably settled on the promotion of *shit* (and along with it *pee*) with splashes of the clinical and cutesy in appropriate places.

Shit is a superb word, really. Sometimes *shit* can be music to my ears. It doesn't have to be spoken in hushed, moralizing tones. SHIT! OH, SHEEIT! A versatile, articulate, and colorful word, it is indeed a pleasure to shout, to roll along one's tongue. A perfectly audible – if not ear-shattering – remarkably ordinary, decent, and modest everyday word.

Furthermore, it is my thought that in legitimately defining *shit*, I might engender some small credibility for the word in anyone still shocked by its usage. *Pee* seems unnecessary to define here, since according to the *Oxford English Dictionary* it is already a euphemism for *piss*. It is also a familiar, cultured sound: We have Ps and peas and appease.

For the too well-bred and the overly delicate, for the betterment of the English language, and perhaps for the next edition of *Webster's*, I offer (it is for the reader to decide whether shamelessly) at the end of the text a complete, unabridged definition of *shit*. For all its subtleties of meaning, this word is extremely unambiguous. *Shit*, in fact, is one of the least misunderstood words in use today.

ANATOMY
OF A CRAP

*Bowels are not exactly a polite subject for
conversation, but they are certainly a
common problem. . . . Please think of me
again as the urologist's daughter. . . . It may
disgust you that I have brought it up at all,
but who knows? Life has some problems
which are basic for all of us – and about
which we have a natural reticence.*

Katharine Hepburn, *The Making of The African Queen*

In the mid-1800s in the Royal Burrough of Chelsea,
London, an industrious young English plumber
named Thomas Crapper grabbed Progress in his pipe
wrench and leapfrogged ahead one hundred years with
a number of sophisticated sanitation inventions.
T.J. Crapper found himself challenged by problems that
we wrestle with yet today; water quality and water
conservation. Faced with London's diminishing reserv-
oirs drained almost dry by the valve leakage and
"continuous flush systems" of early water closets,
Thomas developed the *water waste preventer* – the very
same siphonic cistern with uphill flow and automatic
shut-off found in modern toilet tanks. Thos. Crapper,

T.J. Crapper and his wonderful invention.

Sanitary Engineer, Chelsea (as his name appeared on manhole covers even in Westminster Abbey) was also responsible for laying hundreds of miles of London's connecting sewers – and none too soon. The River Thames had carried such quantities of rotting turds that the effluvium had driven Parliament to convene in the early hours to avoid the vile off-river breeze.

For the Victorian ladies who complained of the WC's hissing and gurgling as giving away their elaborately disguised trips to the loo, Crapper installed the first silencers. Such pretenses as "excuse me m'lord, I must prick the plum pudding" or "I must pick the daises" were foiled when a lady's absence was accompanied by crashing waterfalls and echoing burbles. Among Mr. Crapper's other claims to fame were his pear-shaped toilet seat (the forerunner of the gap-front seat) designed for men, and the posthumous addition to the English language of a vibrant new word: *Crapper!*

Clearly T. J. Crapper was ahead of his day. Progress and time, nonetheless, can be peculiar concepts. Some things in the universe – pollution, the use of euphemisms, *sneaking* off to the bathroom, and tinkling silently down the side of the bowl, to name a few – seem to defy change, even from century to century. But there's been one glaring reversal in regard to crap. Our advanced 1980s populace, well-removed from the novelties and quirks of the first indoor WCs, finds itself having to break entirely new ground, as it were, when relieving itself outside. Ironically, shitting in the woods successfully – that is, without adverse environmental, psychological, or physical consequences – might be deemed genuine progress today. Take Henry, for instance (a namesake, perhaps, or even a descendant of old King Henry VIII).

All the stories you are about to read are true (for the most part), having been extracted from dear friends and voluble strangers on various occasions, sometimes following the ingestion of copious quantities of Jose Cuervo or Yukon Jack. Only the names have been changed to protect the incommodious.

High on a dusty escarpment jutting skyward from camp, a man named Henry, having scrambled up there and squeezed in behind what appeared to be the ideal bush for camouflage, began lowering himself precariously into a deep knee bend. Far below, just out of their bedrolls, three fellow river runners began violating the profound quiet of canyon's first light by poking about the commissary, cracking eggs, snapping twigs, and sloshing out the coffee pot. Through the branches, our pretzel man on the hill observed the breakfast preparations while proceeding with his own morning mission. To the earth it finally fell, round and firm, this sturdy turd. With a bit more encouragement from gravity, it rolled slowly out from between Henry's big boots, threaded its way through the spindly trunks of the "ideal" bush, and then truly taking on a mind of its own, leaped into the air like a downhill skier out of the gate.

You can see the dust trail of a fast-moving pickup mushrooming off a dirt road long after you've lost sight of the truck. Henry watched, wide-eyed and helpless, as a similar if smaller cloud billowed up defiantly below him, and the actual item became obscured from view. Zigging and zagging, it caromed off rough spots in the terrain. Madly it bumped and tumbled and dropped, making its run as though through a giant pinball machine. Gaining momentum, gathering its own little avalanche, round and down it came, spinning like a buried back tire spraying up sand. All too fast it raced down the steep slope – until it became locked into that deadly slow motion common to the fleeting seconds just preceding all imminent, unalterable disasters. With one last bounce, one final effort at heavenward orbit, this unruly escaped goof ball (followed in the same trajectory by an arcing tail of debris) landed in a terminal thud and a rain of pebbly clutter not six inches from the bare foot of the woman measuring out coffee.

With his dignity thus unraveled along sixty yards of descent, Henry in all likelihood might have come home from his first river trip firmly resolved never again to set foot past the end of the asphalt. Of course, left to his own devices and with any determination at all unless he was a total fumble-bum, Henry would have learned how to shit in the woods. Eventually. The refining of his skills by trial and error and the acquiring of grace, poise, and self-confidence – not to mention muscle development and balance – would probably have taken him about as long as it did me: Years.

I don't think Henry would mind our taking a closer look at his calamity. Henry can teach us a lot, and not all by poor example. Indeed, he started out on the right track by getting far enough away from camp to ensure his privacy. It was just that straight up wasn't the best choice of direction. Next he chose a location with a view, although whether he took time to appreciate it is unknown. Usually I recommend a wide reaching view, a landscape rolling away to distant mountain peaks and broad expanses of wild sky. But a close-in setting near a lichen-covered rock, a single wildflower, or even dried up weeds and monotonous talus, when quietly studied can offer inspiration of a different brand.

The more time you spend in the wild, the easier it will be to reconnoiter an inspiring view. A friend of mine calls her morning exercise the Advanced Wilderness Appreciation Walk. As she strides along an irrigation canal practically devoid of vegetation but overgrown with crumpled beer cans, has-been appliances, and rusted auto parts, she finds the morning's joy in the colors of the sunrise and the backlighting of a lone thistle.

But essential for the outdoor neophyte is a breathtaking view. These opportunities for glorious moments alone in the presence of grandeur should be soaked up. They are soul replenishing and mind expanding. And the ideal occasion for communing with nature in this way is while you're peacefully sitting still – yes, shitting in the woods. The rest of the day, unless you're trekking alone, can quickly become cluttered with other social or organizational distractions.

But back to Henry, whose only major mistake was failing to dig a hole. It's something to think about: A small hole may prevent the complete destruction of an ego. A proper hole is of great importance, not only in averting disasters such as Henry's, but in preventing the spread of disease and facilitating rapid decomposition. Chapter Two in its entirety is devoted to *the hole*.

More do's and don'ts for preserving mental and physical health while shitting in the woods will become apparent as we look in on Charles. He has his own notion about clothes and pooping in the wilderness; he takes them off. Needless to say, this man hikes well away from camp and any connecting trails to a place where he feels secure about completely removing his britches and relaxing for a spell. Finding an ant-free log, he digs his hole on the opposite side from the view, sits down, scoots to the back of the log, and proceeds to dream. Remember this one. This is by far the dreamiest, most relaxing set up for shitting in the woods. A smooth, breadloaf-shaped rock (or even your backpack in a pinch in vacant wasteland) can be used in the same manner – for hanging your buns over the back.

This seems like an appropriate spot to share a helpful technique imparted to me one day by another friend: "Shit first, dig later." In puzzlement, I turned to her and as our eyes met, she watched mine grow into harvest moons. But of course "shit first, dig later" – that way you could never miss the hole. Provided you had a shovel for digging and not a stick, it was the perfect solution. Perfect, that is, for someone with bad aim. Me? Not me.

Unlike Charles, there's my longtime friend Elizabeth, who prizes the usefulness of her clothes. While on a rattletrap bus trip through northern Mexico, the lumbering vehicle on which she rode came to a five-minute halt to compensate for the lack of a toilet on board. Like a colorful parachute descending from the desert skies, Lizzie's voluminous skirts billowed to the earth, and she squatted down inside her own private outhouse.

Occasionally it is impossible to achieve an optimal degree of privacy. Some years back, my colleague Henrietta Alice was hitchhiking on the Autobahn in Germany, where the terrain was board flat and barren. At last, unable to contain herself, she asked the driver to stop and she struck out across a field toward a knoll topped by a lone bush. There, hidden by the branches and feeling safe from the eyes of traffic, she squatted and swung up the back of her skirt, securing it as a cape over her head. Henrietta's rejoicing ended quite abruptly. Out of nowhere came a column of Boy Guides (the rear guard?) marching by her bare derrière.

There are many theories on clothes and shitting – all individual and personal. In time you will develop your own. Edwin, no doubt, has a new theory about clothes after one memorable hunting trip; whether it be to take them off or keep them on, I haven't figured out.

For the better part of a nippy fall morning, Edwin had been slinking through whole mountain ranges of gnarly underbrush in pursuit of an elusive six-pointer. Relentlessly trudging along with no luck, he finally became discouraged, a cold drizzle adding to his gloom. Then a lovely meadow opened out before him, its beauty causing him to pause. His attention, now averted from the deer, relaxed into a gaze of pleasure, and he next became increasingly aware of his physical discomforts; every weary muscle, every labored joint, every minuscule bramble scratch – and then another pressing matter.

Coming upon a log beneath a spreading tree, Edwin propped up his rifle and quickly slipped off his poncho, sliding the suspenders from his shoulders. Whistling now, he sat and shat. But when he turned to bury it, not a thing was there. In total disbelief, poor Edwin peered over the log once more but still found nothing. It began to rain, and the pleasant vision of camp beckoned. Preparing to leave, he yanked up his poncho and hefted his gun. To warm his ears, he pulled up his hood. And there it was on top of his head, melting in the rain like so much ice cream left in the sun.

Poor Edwin will not soon forget this day; he walked seven miles before coming across enough water to get cleaned up. Though I fear he was in no humor to be thinking much beyond himself, we can only hope he did not wash directly in the stream. It's important to use a bucket to haul wash water well above the high water line of spring run off, to keep pollutants from entering waterways. But I digress, and this topic is covered thoroughly in the next chapter. For now, back to techniques.

My eighty-six year old uncle cautioned old people fearful of toppling over while squatting (old people, hell) to steady themselves by holding onto a branch or tree trunk. My theory is to find a place to sit: I'm really Charles, the sitting dreamer, in disguise.

If, however, you're a good squatter and also in a hurry, perhaps to chase a caribou or click off pictures of the sunset, you might try a technique perfected by one of our elected U.S. officials. We'll call him Jonathan the Deer Hunter, and, I might add, the Ham. His is a rare performance, an adagio of fluid motion and perfect balance. One night after midnight at the tail end of a venison barbeque bash, I mentioned I was writing this book and received a mock demonstration on the living room rug.

Sinking into a hang ten surfboard pose – knees bent and arms outstretched from the shoulder – Jonathan scrapes a trench four to five inches deep with the heel of one boot (this works only where the earth is fairly soft). Instructing anyone now left in the room, he suggests dropping your jeans (and drops his) either to just below your hips or all the way to your ankles, pointing out that folds of material are uncomfortable when bunched up in the bend at the back of your knee. After squat-straddling the ditch for as long as it takes, he drops in his paper and shoves the excavated dirt back into the trough with the instep side of his boot. In finale, he packs the dirt down the way any good gardener would finish planting a tree. It was a marvelous performance, I had to agree, except for the toilet paper in the hole – the telltale sign of humans on the planet. We'll discuss this later.

From the depths of a lumpy sleeping bag, from the middle of many a wilderness campsite, has come this sort of question, accompanied by a bit of a whine: "Herbert?

Whaddo I do if I have to go in the middle of the night?" Secretly, Herbert might have an identical first-timer question himself, so I'll answer this one for him.

Unless there's a full moon or you have the nocturnal instincts of the snails that go for my petunias, carry a flashlight for those midnight jaunts. As much as I dislike anything resembling civilization when in the boondocks, I concede that in unfamiliar terrain, a tiny light bulb can prevent a stubbed toe, a cracked head – when you trip and pitch over the cliff – or, more commonly, two weeks of the itchy crotch-crazies from lurking poison oak. Many of the contributors to this book have confessed one of those "I hoped I wouldn't live long enough to tell the story" stories. Poison oak seems to be the most common misadventure of night squatting.

One further caution: Carry a *small* flashlight. The searchlight variety is overkill and can predispose the body to more permanent damage from irate fellow campers. There's nothing like waking up in the middle of peaceful nowhere to someone crashing through the bushes with their high beams and a roll of toilet paper.

Observant caution is always the recommended approach in picking out a place to relieve oneself. Poison oak is not the only dastardly culprit abroad. As my friend Ma Prudence Barker notes, one cannot just plop down with wild abandon in any old daisy field – especially a daisy field – and hope to escape unscathed. She once knew a logger named Lloyd who experienced the unequivocal misery of being nailed by a bumble bee smack on the family jewels. Logger Lloyd swore the pain was worse than any chainsaw nick, bullet hole, or careless imprint of spiked Currins Caulk tearing into flesh.

It is prudent to inspect any area for hazards where you're planning to sit down bareassed. Snakes are notorious for sleeping tucked under rocks and logs. Ants run around everywhere. And there are places in the world, as the noted writer and explorer Tim Cahill discovered, where a person can't squat without carrying a big stick to beat off the local pigs. Always check around for damage you might incur. And check for damage you might inflict.

One morning on the Owyhee River in Oregon, our party had already broken camp, loaded the boats, and tied down everything securely and were standing ready to push off into the current when it became apparent to me that the morning's coffee had arrived at the end of its course through my innards.

"Wait, wait," I cried to everyone and raced up the bank. I wound through the jumble of boulders until a convenient rock presented itself. Yanking down my shorts, I sat down and began watering the face of the rock.

Now the southeastern corner of Oregon is home to the chuckar, a relative of the partridge. This chunky, chicken-like bird is saddled with a reputation for being absurdly stupid and the added hereditary misfortune of a lunatic voice. A cuckoo bird with the hiccups couldn't sound sillier. Audubon calls the chuckar a "hardy game bird that can outrun a hunter (first flying uphill, then flying down)." It's been more my experience that if you decide upon chuckar for dinner, you could walk right up to one, hand it a stone, and it would agreeably hit itself over the head for you. Combine the bird's inability for anything resembling graceful flight with its darting, quickstepping motion reminiscent of an old-time movie, add its long hours spent ridiculously burping its own name, and the chuckar becomes a cause for much amusement.

Still propped on the rock, I was appreciating a final glance around one of my favorite river camps and enjoying the pleasure of a shrinking bladder, when there came a loud, crazed *chuk-karr chuk-karr*. A great flapping commotion arose directly from between my knees, convulsed into my face, and then vanished. I knelt down before the wet rock. Tucked beneath a small overhang, behind a clump of grass, I found a precious woven nest holding eight warm eggs – now a lakefront homesite on the edge of a puddle of piss. In one great swoop of karma, all my abusive snickering and pompous guffawing, my enjoyment at the expense of this poor species of fowl, had come home to roost and I felt terrible. Atop a nearby boulder after her fit of apoplexy, the mother remained perplexed, staring at me. While heading back to the beach, I chided the powers that be for not giving me a more acute sense of smell or hearing – in the absence of experience – and resolved to do more vigorous battle with my ignorance.

◆

Most of the foregoing stories are worst-case scenarios. I have recounted them not to scare you out of the woods, but to acknowledge the real perils and suggest how to work around them. Life itself is a risk; you could trip headlong over your own big toe, or you could swallow your breakfast down the wrong pipe, any day of the week. And have you *ever* tried to locate a toilet downtown – a task fraught with more frustration than any possible misfortune outdoors? Someone (not me) really needs to produce instructions for how to shit in the city.

I'll just say this: Disasters of elimination in the city can be more excruciatingly humiliating than those in the bush. Sometimes I think storekeepers, clerks, and tellers all must be terribly regular, "going" at home in the morning and then not needing a *terlit* (as my grandmother from Brooklyn would have said) for the rest of the day. If there *is* a smelly, peeling, wooden seated john tucked away in the far reaches of a dusty storeroom, for some reason this information is as heavily guarded as the most clandestine revolutionary plans. In tramping around town, I've all too often encountered locked doors, scribbled *Out of Order* signs, *Employees Only* plaques, or "I'm sorry we don't have one" fibs. Sometimes, the only recourse is to streak for home and hope to get there in time. I'll take the backcountry, thanks.

So, get on out there. Find a place of privacy, a "place of easement" as the Elizabethans knew it. Find a panoramic view – one that can't be had with a Liberty quarter and the half turn of a stainless steel handle. Go for it!

DIGGING
THE HOLE

Landscape is sacramental, to be read as text.

Seamus Heany

When we try to pick something by itself, we find it hitched to everything else in the universe.

John Muir, *Daily Journal 1869*

Now for the serious stuff. People – corporate lawyers, philandering spouses, presidential candidates – are always wanting to know *how* to bury their shit. This chapter spells out precisely where and how to dig holes that promote rapid decomposition of feces and prevent contamination of waterways, thereby providing the best protection for the health of humans, the remainder of the animal kingdom, and the planet. Before we can hope to fathom how great is the importance of properly digging our own small *one-sit hole* (also termed *cat hole*) in the bush, it's necessary to try to envision our shit in the global sense. *Try* is the trick here.

Exactly where does the world's collective excrement go? Not a pleasant question. How often do any of us think about where it goes after it's sucked down the hole at the bottom of the bowl? Possibly never. Such reflections tend to detour our consciousness, barring those rare occasions when we have to call Roto-Rooter.

Approached from any angle, the actual physical dimensions of this pile of yuck produced upon our globe befuddle imagining. Nevertheless, let's go back to the Mesozoic era and try thinking across the ages – across mountain ranges, across continents – to the present. Let's begin with dinosaur scats.

In all probability, the *Stegosaurus* and *Tyrannosaurus rex* let rip with something roughly the size of a Cadillac. The piles left by the woolly tusked mammoth might have been somewhat smaller, say TR3-size – nonetheless a formidable turd. To the total of the dinosaurs' leavings add the excrement of Cro-Magnon man (and woman) and the wandering tribes. Add the feces of polar bears, black bears, brown bears, gorillas, hippos, and giraffes. Add buffalo chips. Add tiger and rhino dung. Total up the dumps of the Romans (remembering their gluttonous ways), the Vikings (that stout-of-digestion breed), and modern man, woman, and infant (by all means, infant – we know how the human baby goes at it). Include the scats of elephant and lion, deer and antelope, moose and kangaroo, caribou and wallaby. Toss in every species that birdshits – from pterodactyl to parakeet. And finally round up the output of hogs, dogs, horses, cows, rabbits, owls, cats, and rats. In imagining all this, you've put a mere chicken scratch on the surface.

Anyone who's been responsible for the maintenance of a cat's litter box understands how turds have an inherent tendency to pile up like junk mail. And anyone who has skipped across a cow pasture has spent at least a few seconds marveling at the size of those rippled pies (if not sailing the dried ones for frisbees). Now, multiply one – just one – litter box or cow by 230 million years. Gadzooks!

Since the minutest scrap of life began wriggling around on our planet, Mother Earth has been valiantly embracing fecal waste – an astounding display of her natural absorption capacities. An infinitely bottomless garbage pit, however, does not exist. There are times when the amount of waste becomes far too great for it to be amassed comfortably against her bosom. And the amount of the waste can often have less to do with the problem than the manner in which it's discarded.

Take, for instance, all the campers in a national park on one good weather weekend and imagine them as a herd of buffalo corralled in a space the size of your backyard. Or take a boatload of refugees, rolling and tossing, seasick on ocean swells, and visualize them locked for two months inside your favorite movie theater without plumbing. In the absence of properly functioning or adequately dug disposal facilities, accumulated fecal matter rapidly grows into a major sanitation problem, sometimes with devastating consequences. Under such conditions, diseases find king-sized footholds from which to run rampant. Epidemics – not to mention assaults on the aesthetics – are common in regions where the tonnage of yuck exceeds absorption capacities. Fecally transmitted diseases are endemic in most Third World countries, but they are not unheard of in the United States.

Until roughly ten years ago, no one ever considered it unsafe to drink directly from mountain streams. You could stretch out on the bank of a high mountain meadow creek and just push your face into the water to drink. As recently as 1977, the Sierra Club backpacker's guide touted drinking directly from wilderness waterways as one of the "very special pleasures" of backcountry travel. In 1968 Edward Abbey wrote this in Desert Solitaire (new edition, New York: Ballantine, 1985):

> When late in the afternoon I finally stumbled – sundazed, blear-eyed, parched as an old bacon rind – upon that blue stream which flows like a miraculous mirage down the floor of the canyon. I was too exhausted to pause and drink soberly from the bank. Dreamily, deliriously, I waded into the waist-deep water and fell on my face. Like a sponge I soaked up moisture through every pore, letting the current bear me along beneath a canopy of overhanging willow trees. I had no fear of drowning in the water – I intended to drink it all.

But no longer can we *drink it all* – no longer can we drink even a drop before purifying it without running the risk of getting sick. According to the Center for Disease Control in Atlanta, no surface water in the world is guaranteed free of the microscopic cysts responsible for a parasitic disease called *giardiasis*. This is a disease not easily eradicated, either in the wilds or in the human body. Though not fatal, it can be an unpleasant and debilitating illness and, in some cases, chronic. It is also possible to have the disease, show no symptoms but, nonetheless, be a carrier. *Giardiasis* is still a new disease in the medical community and the general public can be instrumental in promoting an awareness of it. To that end, I've reprinted here a list of specific symptoms:

Symptoms of Giardia

1. Sudden onset of explosive diarrhea 7 to 10 days after ingestion (especially in conjunction with wilderness trekking or foreign travel; other sources to consider are domestic dogs and cats and preschool daycare centers).

2. A large volume of foul-smelling, loose (but not watery) stools.

3. Abdominal distention, flatulence, and cramping – especially after eating (most cases begin with this set of symptoms rather than the explosive diarrhea).

4. May include nausea, vomiting, lack of appetite, headache, and low-grade fever.

5. These acute symptoms can last 7 to 21 days, but from there may become chronically persistent or relapsing.

6. In chronic cases, significant weight loss can occur due to mal-absorption.

7. In chronic cases bulky, loose, foul-smelling stools may persist or recur – they may float and be light in color.

8. Chronic symptoms may include flatulence, bloating, consti-pation, and upper abdominal cramps.

9. Chronic infections can last for years and some individuals, unknowingly, are asymptomatic passers of cysts.

[If you think you might have Giardia, you should see a physician for stool testing and to have medication prescribed, though it is thought that most cases resolve spontaneously within 4-6 weeks. Keep in mind that these symptoms are nonspecific; many other intestinal problems can exhibit the same symptoms.]

◆

The actual spread of the Giardia lamblia parasite into the backcountry is an interesting and as yet incom-plete story. Though the particulars of transmission are still under study, it has been determined that strains can be passed between animals and humans. Like many of the world's enteric pathogens (intestinal bugs), Giardia is spread by "fecal-oral" transmission, meaning some form of the infectious organism is shed in feces and enters a new host or victim by way of the mouth. The Giardia lamblia protozoan has a two-stage life cycle. The active stage, the trophozoite, feeds and reproduces in the intestine of the animal host, and any trophozoites excreted in feces die off rapidly. The second stage, the dormant cyst, which is also passed in fecal matter, is much hardier and able to survive in an outside environment.

Direct fecal-oral transmission of *Giardia* cysts is a concern in preschool day care centers and other institutions. This kind of transmission by direct person to person contact (and also transmission via contaminated food) can easily be eliminated in the outback with careful attention to hand washing. It is the waterborne transmission that poses a bigger problem in the wilds. Once the cysts have entered lakes and streams, they can remain viable for months – particularly in cold waters.

Giardia cysts have been discovered in mountain headwaters, the alpine feeders that spring to life from rainfall and eventually wash down to form all our watercourses. Concentrations are higher in some rivers and streams than in others. You might still scoop a pure cupful of water directly from a stream, but the risks aren't worth it. Technically, as soon as water falls from the sky and lands on the ground or bubbles to the surface from a natural spring, it is possible for *Giardia* to be present in it. Only a few cysts need be ingested and enter our intestinal track to cause infection. In "Eat, Drink, and Be Wary" (reprinted from California Wilderness Coalition in *Headwaters*, Friends of the River, March/April 1984), Thomas Suk discusses various paths by which fecal material enters wilderness waterways:

> ...Direct deposition by humans or animals into water, and deposition near water where the cysts can be carried into the water by runoff, rising water levels, erosion, or on the feet of humans or animals. Cysts may also be carried to water on the haircoat of animals who roll in feces.

Giardia is present nowadays in much of the animal kingdom, with strains having been found in fish, birds, reptiles, and thirty mammalian species. Animal feces continually recontaminate remote watersheds. Beavers and muskrats, spending their lives in the water, are known carriers. But the saddest commentary on this disease is that humans may have played the greatest role in spreading it.

Until 1970, there were no reports in the United States of waterborne outbreaks of *giardia*. The first waterborne outbreak occurred in Aspen, Colorado, in 1970. Over the next four years, many cases were documented in travelers returning from, of all places, Leningrad. The explanation for this seems to be a combination of two factors; the Soviet Union became more open to visitation by Westerners at about this time and Leningrad's municipal water supply was full of *Giardia* cysts. The U.S. outbreak sparked debate and speculation, as well as solid ongoing research, into the origins of *giardia* and the manner of transmission among species. Where did it come from? Who gave it to whom? Who bears the greatest responsibility for its spread, animals or humans? What do we do now?

A popular theory, seeming to exonerate humans, is that *giardia* has been around all along – throughout the eons – and is only now beginning to be correctly diagnosed. "Around" appears to be the key word in this theory. *Giardia* may have been around somewhere, but in the Sierras? In the Rockies? Undeniably, there have been reports of *giardia* in other parts of the world since it was discovered in 1681. Personally, I can't help but recall that numerous river cronies and I drank from watersheds all over the western U.S. and Canada throughout the late sixties and into the mid-seventies and never came down with *giardia* – other intestinal disorders on occasion, but not *giardia*. Only in the late seventies and early eighties did we begin to hear repeatedly of unshakable cases of this "new disease" among us.

It seems improbable that we were all previously either asymptomatic carriers or misdiagnosed.

To further humor my personal suspicions as to where the responsibility for the spread of *giardia* lies, I offer a few more thoughts. If left *solely* to the animals in the wild, it seems the progression might have marched along at a different pace, beaver to beaver, stretching over a long period of time – hundreds, even thousands of years (perhaps, never to have reached us at all owing to Darwinian selection or a build up of natural immunities). It is known that both humans and animals can and do spread this disease. There is also evidence to suggest that some animals may rid themselves of *giardia* during the winter months only to be reinfected by humans in the spring.

In the final analysis, in this continuing search to accurately determine the reasons for proliferation, one earnest issue comes to light above all others: It is a matter of grave import for us – animals, such as we are, and possessing a great mental capacity – to try diligently to recognize the potential extent of our impact on the total animal kingdom. Too often we fail to take fully into account the ramifications of our fast-living, expedient ways, which then reverberate through every other aspect of life on the planet – eventually boomeranging to haunt us.

In retrospect, the appearance of *giardia* could be of great benefit to us, if it teaches us only that we are capable of spreading odd, new diseases as fast as we take vacations. Think about it. What animal other than *Homo sapiens* can swallow *rogani gosht* in India or *Kalya e Khass* in South Africa and shit it into the Colorado countryside?

One encouraging report comes from the Department of Conservation in New Zealand. For reasons not altogether clear, many of the wilderness waters in New Zealand have tested negative for Giardia. In fact, New Zealand's Milford Track Association actually encourages hikers to drink directly from streams. The lack of Giardia in New Zealand's remote surface waters may have something to do with that country's strict quarantine regulations on all incoming livestock and pets, the island's inherent isolation, and/or an absence of indigenous water mammals. Whatever the reasons, three cheers for New Zealand! But before running right out to purchase your airline ticket straight to a pure cold slurp of creek water, make certain you finish reading this handbook. Let us not contaminate New Zealand's wild waters!

Permit me one last muse on the global subject of spreading diseases before we take up our trowels to dig holes. In most of Africa and parts of the Middle East and South America, surface waters also are infested with *schistosomes*, the blood flukes that cause *schistosomiasis* (also call *Bilharzia* after the discovering physician). The presence of these flukes precludes any swimming or wading, as their manner of entry is through the skin. Into these waters, Ed Abbey (the late great environmental activist) couldn't dip even his parched big toe to cool off. Fortunately for us in North America, one stage of a *schistosome's* life cycle must take place in a snail found only in the tropics. But who, out there, can promise me that at some future date, a minor mutation in the blood fluke's thermostat might not leave this parasite completely compatible with our temperate zone, garden variety escargot? And if not *Bilharzia*, then something else is bound to arrive (probably already has) upon our shores.

The best line of defense for protecting our wild lands, our wild friends, and ourselves is to develop scrupulous habits of disposal – to dig an environmentally sound hole and bury that shit – and a compulsion for educating newcomers to the woods with a similar fastidiousness.

◆

Now, pick up your backpacker's trowel or old army-entrenching tool and prepare to dig. Choosing a good excavation site for the one-sit hole requires some knowledge and preparation. (The digging of deeper, group latrines is not covered here. Latrine digging instructions are available in many leadership manuals and outdoor training programs.) The objective in digging a hole is to inhibit the passing of disease causing organisms by humans or animals or storm runoff into nearby surface waters and by flying insects back to food areas.

There is no one best set of rules for all terrains, seasons, and climates. In fact, such a collection of variables and trade-offs exists that, at first, it might seem that one would need four PhDs to sort them all out. For example, the decomposition rate of buried fecal material is greatly influenced by all of the following: soil types and textures, filterability (as measured in percolation rates), moisture content, slope of terrain, general exposure, insect inhabitation, pH, and temperature.

The trade-offs in environmental protection are between security and decomposition. The ideal spot for rapid decomposition (rapid is completely relative here; under the best conditions, human shit can take more than a year to vanish) is a dry to somewhat moist – but not excessively moist – area with abundant humus and bacteria. To better understand this description, think of the perfect place as being shaded by some sort of rock formation or vegetation – but not in a drainage area affected by storm runoff or at a site intermittently inundated by an annual rise in water table.

Feces deposited in extremely parched soils in open locations may not be at much risk of removal by runoff. But this kind of ground is difficult to dig into, and the lack of bacterial activity in the meager topsoil could mean that deposits take nigh on forever to decompose. In areas above timberline or in sub-zero climates, sites for holes *must* be chosen with great care for security, as the bacterial activity there is virtually nonexistent. As Chapter Three will show in more detail, under the latter circumstances it is better to pack your poop out – or at least back to where it can be buried in good earth.

If you are interested in becoming an expert or boggling your mind further with all these variables, Harry Reeves has written a fascinating article, "Human Waste Disposal in the Sierran Wilderness" (*Wilderness Impact Studies*. San Francisco: Sierra Club Outing Committee.), reporting the findings of an extensive field study. For the rest of us, one twentieth-century philosopher has stated it well, "One can do *only* what one can do," and so it is with the search for the ideal hole. Our goal, therefore, will be to dig holes that are as ecologically sound and aesthetically pleasing as our layman's knowledge and the rest of this chapter will allow.

The primary consideration in choosing a burial site is to prevent feces from becoming washed into any waterway. Even when buried, the bacteria in human waste is capable of traveling a good distance through the surrounding soil. Choose a location well away from creeks, streams, and lakes – 150 feet is generally recommended, though I find this figure difficult to apply to anything other than lakes. Canyons carved by flowing waterways have vastly different configurations. You can walk away from one for three miles and still remain in the flood plain, while with another you may need to climb only two stories to find a secure spot.

The best plan is to stay above – well above – the high water line of spring runoff. Sometimes this line is not easy to find. A high water line can be as elusive as the other sock – the one you swear went *into* the drier. But with a bit of training, you will be able to find it.

The gush of spring water created by snowmelt usually brings with it a load of debris: gravel, rocks, boulders, brush, limbs, even tree trunks. Invariably, as the flood waters peak, slow, and drop, portions of this debris become caught in the riparian vegetation, settling in a relatively horizontal line. In steep river canyons, as you float along on a late season water level, this line may be stories above your head. You might look skyward in mid-river and notice a lone tree trunk deposited curiously atop a house-sized boulder, so high and dry by midsummer you'd guess only giants could have placed it there.

Another clue to the high water line is a watermark – a bathtub ring – left as a horizontal stain on a canyon's rock walls. Some watercourses rage only in the springtime or during flash floods from thunderstorms and are bone dry the remainder of the year. Learn to develop an eye for terrain and drainages – the low spots, the canyon bottoms, the erosion gullies, the dry washes. Ask knowledgeable locals to acquaint you with how high a river rises during its spring runoff. Gradually, you'll learn to estimate fairly accurately the level from the shape and steepness of a canyon. When in doubt climb higher. Next year might be the cyclical big one – the twenty-five-year flood.

Winter landscapes require more skill. The spring high water line is obliterated under drifts of snow. Terrain is difficult to determine, and the chances of squatting on top of a buried stream bed increase when you are not familiar with an area from previous summer visits. Steer clear of flat, open places, as they may be frozen ponds or wide meadows, the latter being a mountain's flood plains that gather and funnel water into creeks. The best advice is to head for high ground. In deep snowpack or sub-zero temperatures, when you can't dig into the frozen earth or sometimes even dig far enough to find earth, the recommendation is to pack it *all* out. No kidding. More in Chapter Three.

The next and most thankful thing to learn about digging is that you're not required to dig to China. Quite the contrary: The most effective enzymes for breaking down excrement live within the top eight inches of the soil. It's generally recommended that you dig down six to eight inches. This allows sufficient dirt coverage to discourage animal contact and help keep flying insects from vectoring pathogens back to food areas. Sometimes a shovel is more helpful than a small trowel in digging this deeply. Then again, a shovel can disturb more root systems and is heavy to carry. Do your best. The only time you need less coverage is in an actual blazing sand desert. There you can provide just a dusting and let the sun cook the turd to death.

A trekker's urine is an altogether different story. Pee evaporates rapidly and is relatively sterile, unless some sort of bladder infection is present (and a sufferer is usually aware of such a condition). The major caution with peeing is to keep away from high use areas where the stench can become unpleasant. In certain areas, notably Grand Canyon beaches, the National Park Service instructs people to pee directly into the river or on the wet sand at the water's edge; avoid peeing on rocks and gravel where urine leaves a lasting odor. The pee is washed away by the daily fluctuations in water level created by Glen Canyon Dam upstream. These procedures were not adopted just to eliminate rank urine smells; the concentration of pee (and nitrogen) that boaters would otherwise deposit upon the soils of the Grand Canyon – an arid and slow-changing environment – would rapidly alter the soil chemistry. The volume of river water in the Colorado, upwards of 15,000 cubic feet per second, also warrants this practice. Follow this procedure, however, only when the park or forest service specifically requests it.

For *any* type of eliminating, a bush traveler must first wander a good distance from the camp area, not only for privacy, but to avoid squatting on potential sleeping spots or kitchen sites. If you are moving your camp every day, use this to advantage by making deposits in the areas of least visitation along your route. Stay away from trails, which are in themselves high use areas. And plan ahead, or you will find yourself skipping off the trail to the first available nook – one which doubtless had the same appeal to many before you. Certain regions are deep in shit – such as the shores bordering and just upstream of hellbender rapids (Nothing can get it moving faster than thinking you're going to die.).

Let's touch for a moment on the subject of toilet paper. I recently met an ex-rock climber who related the following story. While clinging to a ledge halfway up Yosemite's Half Dome, the urge suddenly came upon her. A point of interest: Rock climbing is the least regulated of outback activities, and rock climbers are notorious for just letting it fly, bombs away! It's not uncommon to hear stories of climbers who've gotten hit on the head. But in this instance, the climber was organized to be respectful of the mountain and other climbers. Remaining safely in her leg loops, she skillfully peeled down her pants and positioned the plastic bag she carried. Next, she ripped off an arms length of toilet tissue, then somehow let go of it, and it floated away. The paper curled downward for a only moment before being snatched by an updraft. For the better part of an hour, soaring, diving, looping, happy as a mime artist, it entertained everyone strung across Half Dome. Need I say more about hanging onto your t.p.?

Actually, yes, two more cautions. Don't bury it. Don't burn it. Burning has been the accepted practice for some years, but the thinking on this is now changing. No matter how careful you think you may be, one accidental forest fire is one too many. Use as little paper, therefore, as you can manage and then *pack it all out.* To better encourage this practice when camped with others, it's helpful to provide instructions and a discreet location for collection. A collection bag (paper, if it is to be burned in a campfire) can be stationed at the outer edge of camp along with a shovel (most backpackers carry their own trowels) and a roll of t.p.

It goes without saying that you should also pack out all the other inorganic accouterments of toiletry: tampons, sanitary pads, and diapers. Should you be washing diapers on a trip, dispose of the actual ca-ca in one-sit holes dug in the manner previously described. Haul the wash bucket above the high water line; use only biodegradable soap. In rinsing out the wash bucket, use another pan or bucket to avoid rinsing directly in a stream. Pour the water into a hole (again, above the high water line) and cover with dirt.

◆

Ocean saltwater is a different story than fresh water. It is customary when sea kayaking to void in a can, toss the contents overboard, rinse out the can, and resume paddling. Or, if it is warm enough, you can just jump overboard – provided you are practiced in solo rescue and can get back in. On ecological grounds some sea touring groups actually recommend water disposal over waiting for a beach disposal.

On first thought the idea of depositing one's excretia in water ran contrary to all environmental fibers in my being. An experience awhile back in Mexico reinforced this resistance. Someone once handed me a cheap ticket to Acapulco. I arrived on the lovely tropical beaches only to be warned not to go swimming in the polluted bay waters – too much raw sewage, it seemed. When the heat became oppressive, I swam in the hotel's chlorinated pool – kind of like being at the Y at home. As you might understand, then, it is with undying reluctance that I put forth these poop and dump procedures for ocean kayakers. Nevertheless, I have been informed that the ocean is quite capable of breaking down a few turds.

A kayak, after all, is but a one-person/one-coffee can yacht. If you consider the number of sea kayakers bobbing around in a vast ocean, then dumping out your can in the water seems a fair practice. I promise, I won't worry about it. I'll worry about the Queen Mary-sized cruise ships flushing their holding tanks, about coastal towns worldwide running raw sewage into the sea, about oil spills, about barrels of toxic waste, about balloons turning up in dead marine animals' intestines, about the price of scallops. . . and such. That's enough to worry about.

I don't suppose anyone will be attempting the first of these water disposal maneuvers (using the can) within sight of a crowded beach, since the balance and verve of an Olympic pommel horse performer are required to shit in a can while floating in a kayak, not to mention what's needed if you're wearing a wet suit. In any case, whether you use a can or jump overboard, it's only sensible to stay away from small bays, harbors, and any beaches where sludge might wash ashore before breaking up. And both of these techniques require practice – dry runs, so to speak – in calm waters at home. Indeed, you have a valuable companion when someone will steady your boat for you while gallantly refusing to peek. Should you be planning to paddle a two-seater – unless you're unruffable and endowed with great panache – better hope you draw the rear seat. As you would with any new camp practice – setting up a tent, for instance – test it out with your partner before setting out to sea, like the Owl and the Pussycat in your beautiful pea-green boat.

WHEN YOU CAN'T DIG A HOLE

In days of old
When knights were bold
And toilets weren't invented,
They left their load
Along the road
And walked off so contented.

A childhood ditty; author unknown

In the pursuit of unknowns, a ranging world explorer can throw open entire new universes, not to mention some curious dimensions of toiletry and disposal. Sometimes there's just no place to dig a hole. Most of us never have occasion to pray that we won't have to go big potty outside when it's forty below or while dangling in midair between pitons on a hundred-foot rock face. In all probability, we are home knitting or walking the dog. Of course, anyone trudging on foot to the South Pole or climbing Mount Everest is already committed to a multitude of unpleasantries. These breeds of outdoor enthusiasts are extraordinary souls;

pride in their accomplishments does not spring from enduring the ordinary. The morning constitutional behind the morning paper is an ordinary, even enjoyable, task when performed at home. But under adverse conditions, a simple activity can become a colossal calamity or feat of contortion. Consider the mishap Chris Bonington endured at 26,000 feet during an ascent on Everest, as described in his book *The Ultimate Challenge* (New York: Stein & Day, 1963):

> Now we've got these one-piece down suits; it's not too bad, in fact it's comparatively easy to relieve oneself when wearing the down suit by itself. If, however, you are wearing the down suit and the outer suit, it is absolutely desperate, trying to get the two slits to line up. . . . Afterwards, without thinking, without looking back, I stood up and shoved my windproof suit back on. . . . I did not realize anything was wrong – until I poked my hand through the cuff! I tried to scrape it off – rub it off – but by this time the sun had gone, it was bitterly cold and it had frozen to the consistency of concrete.

And take note of this poor woman, who also bought a suit of misery. A demented (an interpretation of the explorer's term *robust*) friend of mine was camped on Oregon's Three Sisters during a blizzard when an imperious peristaltic contraction indicated it was time to crawl out of the tent and squat. So she crawled out, into a complete whiteout, with snow blowing horizontally on a wicked wind. Five layers of clothes had to be stripped from her rosy behind and shoved below her knees. Never mind freezing, in retrieving her pants she found that each layer, not unlike a bird bath, had captured a supply of snow. Once the clothes were clasped to her body again, the snow began to melt. Winter campers call it the "soggies." When questioned as to whether she might not have some helpful hint for others caught in such circumstances, her only reply came, "Hold it!"

Yet two timeworn solutions to the undeniable problems associated with winter camping do offer themselves. Trap doors decidedly provide some buttress against inclement weather. Fashioned after the old union suits with their buttoned fanny drop-flaps, various styles are now available in heavy expedition wear. Bonington's predicament may provide a little solace after the fact – in the misery-loves-company category – or might at least serve to forewarn you of one disastrous route to humiliation.

And the other merciful aid in sub-zero temperatures? Just what did great grandmother do when it was too bitter to pad along in her bare feet and flannel nightie to the outhouse? Of course: The old porcelain chamber pot – the thunder mug as it was called. Less elegantly, coffee cans, plastic bags, and a variety of other containers have been used. A friend, an expedition leader, was caught in rush hour gridlock on the fourth level of a freeway interchange. Fortunately it was only a Number One emergency; he filled his thermos four times, casually dumping the contents out the window. Also, I understand from another reliable source that Tupperware bread savers have been put to the same good use on long cross-country hauls across barren landscapes.

◆

As I sit here tapping out this chapter on a state of the art computer, hundreds of barrels of frozen turds and urine lie around McMurdo Station, Antarctica – looking for a home. The general garbage situation in McMurdo, our major U.S. South Pole science station, is an "unseemly story," a mountain "hideous to behold," as the *San Francisco Examiner* reports. By the time you read this chapter – who knows – some of these barrels may very well be thawing in your own home town.

If the world is to survive the onslaught of use (misuse) and overuse in the coming years, we must find better means for disposing of human waste. The number of both hardy explorers and more casual wilderness travelers continues to swell around the globe – and so does the volume of shit. In many respects, we're still grappling with the identical sanitation problems of T.J. Crapper's nineteenth century. Too much stuff, no good place for it to go. No matter how scrupulous people are becoming (and in some areas they are) in packing out garbage to the major trailheads – each wave still leaves behind footprints and poop. You can only cram so many apples in a barrel and then the barrel is full.

A burgeoning feeling in the outdoor community is that we can no longer afford – like knights of old – to leave our load along the road. One example, becoming grievously noticeable to early spring backpackers, is the human waste of the previous season. After the snows melt, the frozen brown lumps of winter's cross-country skiers are left sitting on top of the ground. As the weather warms, they thaw and ripen along with the rest of the landscape.

Interest is growing in a viable inoffensive procedure for getting an individual traveler's fecal matter back to the trailheads. *Groups* of wilderness travelers have been addressing this problem for years. The River Permit Office for the Grand Canyon issues two full pages of instructions for packing out a group's Porta-Potty contents. Since 1979 all solid human waste from Grand Canyon river trips has been containerized and packed out in watertight boxes. No trip is allowed on the river without ample containers, proper education, and a vowed commitment to *pack it all out*. The same is true on other heavily used rivers.

River trips have posed a unique problem in that most of the traffic is naturally confined along the beaches in narrow canyons. The concentration of travelers has been followed quite rapidly by a tremendous build-up in fecal matter. The need to *pack it out* becomes evident when people begin turning over someone else's "stuff" in an effort to bury their own.

As more places in the wilds are overrun with use comparable to river canyons, more packing it out will be required. Cal Adventures, the outdoor program at the University of California at Berkeley under the direction of Rick Spittler, has been experimenting with an individual *pack it out* system for skiers in their winter cross-country program. Their offering of a spring backpackers program no doubt spurred the development of this system. For chamber pots they use plastic bags, double bagging for safety. Admittedly, the concept of carrying around warm shit in your backpack is not just revolutionary; at first thought, it's overwhelmingly repulsive. Only if you're lucky will the weather be cold enough to freeze it. To get past the involuntary "gak!" reaction, it helps if you look upon the whole procedure as one of the marvels of nature; the shrinkage of food supply as the poop container fills. When we deal this intimately with our own volume of excrement, we cannot escape a firsthand, eye-opening reflection on the magical powers of Mother Nature.

◆

Let's consider the whens and hows of *packing it out* when hole digging is impossible or nonecological. This procedure is recommended for rock climbers (those uncouth beasts), for those camping in severe winter conditions (when you can't find any dirt or you'd rather stay in the tent), and for visitors to high use areas in the effort to keep those sites looking pristine. Understandably, rock climbers have the toughest time given the added acrobatics involved in keeping a mountain clean. What can I say? Practice. Take your plastic bags and twisties and hang off the patio tree.

In the snow, a plastic bag is easy to use. Just scoop out a small, deep hole in the snow and line it with the plastic bag. Then sit down. If it's too cold, carefully rest your buns upon your gloves. A plastic bag can also be your chamber pot inside a tent; this will be a breeze, provided you know your fellow campers well enough. If you're desperate enough, who cares; or, better yet, send *them* into the blizzard. Inside, it's sometimes easier to kneel, particularly if you're not an accomplished squatter. Kneel with your knees somewhat apart and your heels farther apart in a comfortable position. Hold the bag with one hand in front of you and one hand in back. Double bag the result and tuck it into a snowbank until morning.

There is also the milk carton, which has some advantages. Unlike a plastic bag, a milk carton will stand up on its own. It becomes the better container when you lack snow to support a bag. First you squat and do what you must; then with your trowel or shovel, scrape up a bit of snow or dirt to go with the load and toss it into the carton. The other advantage is the added sturdiness of the carton inside your backpack. Be sure to duct tape the lid tightly closed between uses. The milk carton is also easier to handle back at the trailhead where it must part ways with its contents.

The trailhead facilities require a few words. Right here, at the trailhead, there is a large gap in the disposal process. After painstakingly hauling your human waste out of a wilderness camp, you will often find there are no facilities nearby that are equipped to receive it.

When I began asking around, it was not uncommon to hear woeful tales from frustrated river runners who, at the completion of a trip, felt doomed to driving a vehicle permanently laden with bagsful of shit. Many a moonless landscape, a handy dumpster, or a lonesome spot in the road have caught their share of "fling it and runs." There is something terribly awry when the most environmentally dedicated bunch is stuck with no better solution. Reputable outfitters generally make arrangements to empty their containers at recreational vehicle sites or sewage treatment plants, though these may be a long haul from their base of operations. Private groups and individuals also need to plan ahead.

Once you arrive at a proper waste dump facility you will discover that they are not set up to receive plastic bags, so be prepared to pour our the contents of your container. At R.V. dumps you will need a large funnel to direct the matter into a small pipe. Plastic bags floating around in treatment plants wreck havoc as they do not decompose for a long time. And formaldehyde, which is an ingredient in many Porta-Potty additives, inhibits the bacterial activity necessary for proper breakdown. Sewage treatment plants recommend using an organic bacterial additive. There are several brands on the market and they are most readily found at R.V. camps. *R.V. Trine* is one such natural enzyme waste digester and it is available at KOA camps.

The individual hiker has the easiest time with final disposal, being able in most places to head directly to the trailhead outhouses, or even home. More often than not, as we roll into the 1990s, the old one-holers sit atop concrete holding tanks that are periodically pumped out by a visiting honey wagon. Again, plastic bags (or cartons) will gum up the works by plugging up the pump. Therefore, dump only the contents down the hole; then seal the container tightly. Because the discarding of this container is the weak link in the system, it is worth double or triple bagging it before tossing it in the trash.

We've made a fine start hauling human waste out of the wilderness; only a few glitches remain on the urban end. In the long run, it remains unclear whether this glaring gap in trailhead disposal facilities needs to be addressed by the forest service and the national park system, the sanitation districts, or some change in state laws.

◆

Our wild lands shrink, our urban lifestyles manufacture more madness, and our need to touch nature increases. More overuse is directly ahead of us. It's easy to see in the simple arithmetic of numbers of *one-sit holes* that *packing it out* will expand the limits of visitation in high use areas. Misuse on top of overuse further narrows the territory of enjoyable wild terrain. In essence, a shrinking wilderness means more warm shit in your backpack! (A little something to remember the next time your vote is needed for preservation.) Trust me, the *individual* Porta-Potty is the backwood's tsunami of the future and a small price to pay to preserve what little is left. If you turn out to be a little queasy about the foregoing process of removal, take comfort in the thought that you won't be alone – either in feeling queasy or in *packing it out*. Until a sweet-smelling, biodegradable method of containerization appears on the market, grab your plastic bag, hold your nose (if it helps), and take your shit with you when you leave.

TREKKER'S
TROTS

*Lomotil, lomotil, wherefore art thou, my
lomotil?*

Anonymous traveler in Puerto Vallarta

During the violent shaking of an earthquake, a
solid, earth-filled dam can turn into liquid and
wash away. Trekker's trots is a similar phenomenon
occurring within the intestinal walls of the mammalian
body. I've seen it happen to my Clydesdales during
Fourth of July fireworks celebrations at the county fair.
Seconds after the first cannon blasts, the horses are
dispersing streams of green alfalfa soup. When this
instantaneous liquefication happens in the species
homo sapiens, we call it: *turista, Montezuma's revenge,*
the *green apple two-step*, or, quite simply, the *shits*.

Such a watery biological response can be brought
about by any number of things besides flus and other
diseases. Our immune systems grow up where we do,
leaving our resistances unequipped for various foreign
foods and water. Traveling itself can be overwhelming;
changes in climate, altitude, and time zone take their
toll on the human system. The anxiety of making all –
or missing half – of your travel connections can have

anyone reaching for Riopan Plus and Kaopectate. Or the sheer fright of an adventure just a bit too thrilling can "set it off" faster than a shaken beer exits its container. Two of my favorite friends seem to be hit by this particular disorder whenever they set foot inside an airport; thus, they have coined another modern euphemism, "airporters," for that most dreaded of afflictions, traveler's diarrhea.

This short chapter – short as I hope all your bouts with this subject will be – emphasizes prevention. Once you've been struck by an airporter, there isn't a whole lot to be said – only to resist cleaning up in a nearby creek and remember to do any washing above the high water line. It helps to have a good friend in this sort of situation – someone to bring you wash water and clothes and offer comfort. Someone who won't hold their sides and laugh at your condition.

Focusing on prevention automatically brings us face to face with sanitation practices once again. Since enteric pathogens (the intestinal bad guys) are transmitted by various forms of fecal-oral contact, logically, then, the first step toward prevention is to ritualize hand washing. Get yourself and all your traveling companions into the habit of washing *after* squatting and *before* preparing food or eating. Be neurotic about it! On a commercial river trip, at each camp the guides set up a bucket of water, a bar of soap, and a cup or longhandled ladle near the group Porta-Potty. The ladle is for scooping water out of the bucket, so you don't contaminate the clean water by thrusting your hands into it. If you're traveling in your own group without a Porta-Potty, you can set up this same washing arrangement at the edge of camp in the area where you station the shovel, toilet paper, and refuse bag. I can't stress enough the importance of hand washing for outdoor people who tend to equate ruggedness – that messing and sweating about in earth's fresh fragrant dirt – with the *primeval*, the long sought-after excuse not to bathe for days.

Another precaution against the shits is to watch what you eat and drink. Properly refrigerate perishable foods and carefully disinfect all drinking, cooking, and food washing water. The treatment of wilderness water against infectious organisms is termed *field water disinfection*. Enteric pathogens come in three main categories: parasitic cysts, bacteria, and viruses. *Giardia* cysts are widespread and must be considered a hazard everywhere in the world. In the U.S. and Canada, problematic bacteria can not be called epidemic, but they turn up occasionally and seem to be on the increase. In other parts of the world, particularly in developing countries, field water and even municipal water supplies must be treated against bacteria, and most importantly, against viruses.

Any number of filter systems on the market will effectively remove protozoan cysts. To varying degrees, the same systems will disinfect for bacteria. A filter with a maximum pore size of 5 microns will remove *Giardia*; a filter of .2 microns will remove all bacteria as well. At the time of this writing, filter systems provide no protection against viruses. The acceptable choices to date to remove viruses are iodine, chlorine, and boiling, and they all have their drawbacks.

A few suggestions on different methods of field water disinfection: If you are headed into the Canadian or U.S. interior for a vacation of average length, you won't need to invest in anything more expensive than one of the charcoal filter and pump systems. The **Water One** ($39.95; replacement filter $27.50, from Calco Ltd., 7011 Barry Ave., Rosemont, Ill. 60018) has a 30 to 50 micron prefilter that will remove some filter-clogging debris, and a .5 micron filter that will remove *Giardia*. The inlet strainer is weighted to stay under the surface to prevent air and large particles from entering the cartridge. It comes with a dye for testing the filter's integrity and has a 400-gallon capacity. The hand bulb pump, which can also be worked with your foot, can be backwashed to unclog the filter. The **First Need** ($39.95; replacement filter $24.95, from General Ecology, Inc., 151 Sheree Blvd., Lionville, PA 19353) has a .4 micron filter, an intake strainer to keep out debris, and a 90 to 160-gallon capacity, depending on the turbidity of the water. With a recent additional attachment to the pump, it can now be easily operated by one person, and be backwashed to unclog. The pre-filter, recommended to lengthen the life of the filter, costs an added $6.50. The First Need apparatus is a little lighter and less cumbersome than the Water One. It removes *Giardia* and some bacteria and can be operated by one person. The **Timberline** ($24; replacement filter $12, from Timberline Filter, P.O. Box 12007, Boulder, CO 80303) is an alternative to the charcoal filter. It's appreciated by backpackers for the minimal weight (6 ounces) and is surprisingly sturdy for its appearance. The Timberline's 2 micron, fiberglass/polyethylene matrix filter disinfects only for *Giardia*. When plugged, the hand pump can either be back flushed or replaced. An identical outfit to Timberline is marketed under the brand name **Coghlan** (from Coghlan's Ltd. Winnipeg, Manitoba R3T 4C7 Canada).

If your intentions are to travel for an extended period of time, or if you head off to the woods regularly, a **Pocket Katadyne** ($170; replacement filter $90, from Water Quality Inc., P.O. Box 1871, Boulder, CO 80306) is a worthwhile investment. The ceramic filter can last as long as six years with active use, thereby making up the frequent replacement costs of the less expensive outfits. The Katadyne's .2 micron pores effectively remove all bacteria and cysts. The Katadyne is the Mercedes of filter systems; for the hard-core outdoor folks, it is the way to go.

Overseas travel requires additional methods of disinfecting for viruses. The oldest method is simply boiling. Contrary to previous thinking, *boiling* is now thought to kill *all* waterborne enteric pathogens *immediately*. Lengthening the boiling time for higher altitudes seems to be unnecessary. Dr. Howard Backer, M.D. and lecturer at U.C. Berkeley, has written a comprehensive article entitled "Field Water Disinfection" for the 1989 edition of *Management of Wilderness and Environmental Emergencies* (Edited by Auerbach and Geehr. St. Louis, Baltimore, Toronto: C.V. Mosby.) This is a mammoth medical book, $117, full of fascinating articles but not written for the layperson. On the basis of new studies, Dr. Backer reports that any water is adequately disinfected by the time it reaches the boiling point – even at altitudes of 24,000 feet where the boiling point is as low as 74.5°C. The major drawback of relying solely on boiling for disinfection is in lugging around enough fuel to accomplish the job.

The chemical disinfectants, *chlorine* and *iodine* (called halogens), are the other choices for eliminating viruses from water. Chlorine is the preferred disinfectant for municipal water supplies and iodine has been used by the military since the beginning of the century. Though halogens work well on viruses and bacteria, parasitic organisms have a higher resistance. For wilderness travelers, one added precaution is to filter/disinfect for *Giardia* prior to halogenating.

The average backcountry traveler is confronted with a confusing array of halogen forms. Halogens come as chlorine (halozone) tablets, ordinary household liquid bleach, iodine crystals, tincture of iodine, and saturated solutions of iodine. The stability of halozone tablets is questionable. Always buy a new bottle before each trip and keep it tightly sealed and out of the heat. You must be mindful of the corrosive effects of all halogens, particularly of carelessly handled iodine crystals. Halogens do not disinfect properly when prepared in insufficient concentrations or without allowing the necessary contact time. Higher pH, lower temperatures, and cloudy water all decrease effectiveness. Also, certain organic and inorganic contaminants may chemically combine with the halogens to decrease a carefully measured out concentration. And then there is the terrible chemical flavor that is objectionable, though less so in lower concentrations. A few medical cautions are to be observed with iodine: Do not use iodine when pregnant or if you have iodine sensitivity or thyroid disease. Iodine alters the results of thyroid functioning tests.

If you decide on one of the iodines, **Polar Pure** ($9.75; from Polar Equipment, 12881 Foothill Lane, Saratoga, CA 95070) is a new product with a trap inside the bottle to safely contain the crystals. Use warm water and carefully follow the standard recommendations, allowing as much contact time as you can to lessen the amount of chemical. When treating cloudy water, you can pre-filter the water through cheesecloth or a coffee paper: By decreasing the amount of junk in the water, you reduce the halogen demand and it will taste better. Or *after* disinfecting with a halogen, you can pump the water through a charcoal filter again to remove the dreadful chemical flavors.

One good option is the **Sierra Water Purifier** ($12.95 starter kit, from Four in One Water Systems, 142 Lincoln Ave., Suite 701, Sante Fe, NM 87501), a new idea in chlorination. It's a two-step operation. First you *super*-chlorinate, killing all microorganisms. Then you add hydrogen peroxide, which chemically combines with the chlorine making plain old H_2O again and a few innocuous salts. A supply of SWP capable of treating 160 gallons is still compact and lightweight, and the price is right. It tastes like water!

◆

Back in the sixties on a plane to Mexico, I remember clutching – with the preoccupation of a small girl with a cuddly blanket and separation anxiety – a bottle of tiny white lomotil tablets. Lomotil was all that a general practitioner in those days knew to recommend. Today, travel medicine has become a speciality, called *emporiatrics*. A network of travel clinics strung across the country provides pre-trip immunizations, offers informational handouts written for Mary Q. Public, suggests appropriate prophylactic medications, and diagnoses post-trip ailments (most people will have returned home by the time *giardia* symptoms first appear).

In general, prophylactic medications for mild cases of *turista* are not recommended for healthy travelers since medications can get in the way of diagnosis and treatment if you come down with something serious. The exception to this is Pepto-Bismol which has been recommended as the latest preventive and cure. Consult your physician prior to foreign travel about using Pepto-Bismol.

If trekker's trots does get you, it is critical to maintain your hydration. This can usually be accomplished orally (provided you're not also throwing up) by drinking alternate eight-ounce glasses of:

1. Orange, apple, or any fruit juice rich in potassium with ½ teaspoon of honey or corn syrup and a pinch of salt.
2. Water with ¼ teaspoon baking soda.

In addition to washing hands and disinfecting water, there are a few other easily followed preventative tactics. In Third World countries, it helps to stay away from "ground-grown" vegetables, especially leafy greens that may have been contaminated by soil, washing water, or dirty hands. A handout entitled *Traveler's Diarrhea*, put out by the University of Connecticut Health Center, reminds us, "if you can't boil it, cook it, or peel it, then forget it!" Addresses for other helpful resources are listed below. Don't forget to disinfect dishes and utensils by using (biodegradable) soap and a strong-smelling chlorinated rinse. Allow them to air dry rather than reducing the contact time by wiping dry with a towel.

Remember all this and you will avoid most cases of trekker's trots, as long as you don't stumble out of the jungle into a colorful roadside cafe and order yourself a bottled soda with contaminated ice!

◆

Directory of Clinical Consultants in Tropical Medicine, Medical Parasitology, and Travelers' Health. This is a list of physicians who are members of the American Society of Tropical Medicine and Hygiene. Most are located in the U.S.; a few are overseas. The directory is offered as a public service and you can obtained one by sending an 8½ x 11 SASE with $.90 U.S. postage to Dr. Leonard Marcus, 148 Highland Ave., Newton, MA 02160. International travelers are advised to seek medical advice six weeks before departure dates, so plan accordingly.

Center for Disease Control, Division of Quarantine, Atlanta, Georgia, (404) 639-2572. The CDC is a government agency under the U.S. Department of Health and Human Services with information on endemic diseases worldwide. They provide the public with recommendations and requirements for immunizations – by country – for foreign travel. You may be able to avoid a long distance call by first contacting your local county public health department or one of the CDC's Public Health Service Quarantine Stations located in Chicago, Los Angeles, Honolulu, Miami, New York, Seattle, or San Francisco.

Health Hints for the Tropics, 9th edition, (approximately $2), available from the Secretary/Treasurer of the American Society of Tropical Medicine and Hygiene, currently William A. Sodeam, Shreveport, LA 71130-3932. This publication should be available from any of the doctors in the *Directory* (above), who generally stock this book for their patients.

The Travel and Tropical Medicine Manual, Elaine C. Jong, M.D.($19.95, Philadelphia: W. B. Saunders Company, 1987) This book covers every foreign disease imaginable if you can struggle through the medical terminology.

The Pocket Doctor, Stephen Bezruchka ($2.95, Seattle,WA: The Mountaineers) A small and more general book for the outdoor addict. It has a good bibliography and a range of odd topics like "hotel fires" and "wild animal attacks" (which to know about might ward off a good case of the *shits*).

An Explorer's Handbook: An Unconventional Guide for Travelers to Remote Regions, Christina Dodwell, ($12.95, New York: Facts on File, 1986). This one is a favorite of mine for the international bush traveler. With such topics as how to stare down a leopard, how to catch, skin, and cook a crocodile, how to outsmart bush bandits, it is worth reading for pleasure or as an aid to real survival.

Infectious Diarrhea From Wilderness and Foreign Travel, a second article by Howard Backer, M.D., in *Management of Wilderness and Environmental Emergencies*, 1989 edition, Auerbach and Geehr eds., C.V. Mosby. Highly informative, covers *giardia* , but not written for the layperson.

Health Advice for International Travel, David R. Hill, M.D. and Richard D. Pearson, M.D., Annals of Internal Medicine, Vol. 108; No. 6 (June 1988). "This review will provide the rationale to determine which vaccines, prophylactic medications, and other preventive measures are appropriate for persons visiting the developing world." Understandable to a layperson.

How to Stay Healthy Abroad: An authoritative guide for the international traveler, Richard Dawood, M.D. ($8.95, New York: Viking Penguin, 1988) Order from Gordon's Books, Inc., 2323 Delgany Street, Denver, CO 80216 or phone (800) 525-6979; in Colorado call (800) 332-6351. A must for individual travelers wanting to make intelligent decisions about their own health.

McVey '89

FOR
WOMEN
ONLY: HOW
NOT TO PEE
IN YOUR
BOOTS

The significance of my position was the opportunity for my growth.

Valerie Fons, *Keep It Moving*

A chapter for women. Why not? I've been a female all my life, as many pairs of soggy socks, jaundiced sneakers, and rancid leather boots can attest. Men need no pointers on how to pee. Men can pee while maintaining the decorum of a three-piece-suiter strolling down Park Avenue. To whizz, men just find a tree, not to hide behind but to lean on while pondering the goings-on of the universe – one hand propped high on trunk, the other aiming the penis. With backs turned but in full view of the world, men piss for anyone present, sometimes in baronial silhouette against a blazing sunset, sometimes without a break in the conversation, as if the flaunting of their ritual were the greatest part of its pleasure. Women, on the other hand, search for a place to hide (god forbid anyone should know we have to pee in the first place) where with panties dropped and sweet asses bared, we must assume the position of a flustered duck trying to watch itself pass an egg.

Possibly Freud deserves more credit than I normally grant him. Though I don't remember a childhood Oedipal complex, in adulthood there have been occasions when, along with the urge to pee, I've been seized by a fierce penis envy. But cheer up, my dears, the rest of this chapter is just for us. With a little practice we, too, can cultivate the ultimate in blasé, while being proud of a challenge faced and won, a job well done. (Not just a piddling vaingloriousness in the operation of an appendage come by genetically!)

As a rule, men pee with dignity, it might even be said with class; sometimes with machismo alone, but always with ease. Except when troubled by the inclement conditions reflected in the time-honored proverb, Never into the Wind, men, by and large, are carefree pee-ers. It's high time women peed with a similar sense of pride and had as much fun.

Had I paid more attention when I was growing up in the forties and fifties, my grandmother might well have been my illustrious peeing mentor. Now, I have only a remembrance of accompanying her into public restrooms. Hoisting her skirts, she would slip one leg out of her wide-legged underdrawers, twist them around the other leg to hold them outstretched matador-fashion, and then with the shuffle of a too tightly reined horse, back bowlegged over the bowl and fire away. In those days, I had no time for this bizarre old-fashioned method: I was too busy balancing little bits of folded paper all around the seat (as my mother had taught me), half of which ended up on the floor from the slight breeze caused by my turning around to sit down. Finding with regularity that a person could water her pants before successfully executing this preparation, I eventually gave it up and just sat down. It was my ignorant but expedient theory that if everyone else were following this ridiculous paper procedure, the seat surely must be free from whatever frightful diseases were to be avoided – diseases never explained, only alluded to mysteriously.

To this day, except where sanitary seat tissues ("butt gaskets" in some circles) are furnished for resting upon, I have yet to master a reliable restroom technique. Sometimes I try bracing myself against the stall's walls, toilet tank, or paper dispenser, or even hanging onto the doorknob (if there is one) in an effort to suspend my bum an inch above the seat. About then I remember a couple of friends: One who lets herself in and out of cubicles with a piece of Kleenex and flushes public toilets with her shoe rather than come into skin contact with those germ-ridden levers; and another, a man, who choreographs an elaborate routine for escaping the men's room without touching a thing. Unnerving me further while seated on a sanitary cover, is this idle question: If the last person's pee can soak through this thin tissue shield, what else might there be swimming through? Oh, grandmother and baggy underwear, where are you now?

Fortunately, out in the bush we face none of these civilized problems. Give me peeing in the woods any day. Once you get the hang of it, it's a blissful refreshing experience. After a long outdoor stint, I find I'm severely depressed with the cold, white, closed-in ambiance and flushing racket of even my home bathroom.

In Third World countries, another stand-up peeing style (outshining even my grandmother's) is performed by women who grow up unhampered by underwear. The secret lies somewhere in the tilt of the pelvis and the near bowing of the femurs, which allow peeing with Olympian accuracy. All is made easier by practice since toddler age and the attire of skirts.

Today women think of skirts as less than functional in the woods; but the fact that men were originally assigned pants and women skirts, was, in all probability, due not to high fashion but to sheer biological practicality. Someone could make a fortune by designing pants for women with a comfortable velcro-closing crotch.

If you should so desire, don't hesitate to scramble the outbacks in a dirndl or sarong as Robyn Davidson, the author of *Tracks* (New York: Pantheon Books, 1980), wore crossing the Australian desert with her camels. "Whatever works" is a good philosophy. When we pass on the trail, I'll recognize another independent, experimental spirit. Who can tell? Someday even our inhibitions about crotch exposure might evaporate in a revolution similar to "ban the bra," bringing us full circle to a resurrection of the bare-bottomed leopard skin mini! For practical reasons.

I should mention that it is possible to master a stand-up peeing technique if clothed in a pair of loose-fitting shorts – by sliding the crotch material to one side. One friend does this and then squats; but another woman I know can adjust the material and stand right along a roadside to pee. If, in driving by, you miss seeing her stream, you might guess she was only stretching her legs and soaking up the view. Practice is the secret, they say. I am going to practice.

But right now, back to wearing shorts, jeans, and bikini underwear, where the process of peeing becomes limited to sitting or squatting. Squatting was never one of my best shots; the liquid soon puddled up and spattered onto everything within three feet. In addition, I have a lousy sense of balance. With all muscles in tight concentration, my success at relaxing just the few correct ones to facilitate peeing without toppling over is comparable to my luck on the slot machines: A jackpot once in a lifetime. I tend to reserve the stamina required for these feats for the few times when nothing but sand dunes stretch as far as the bladder can see.

Slowly, I recognized that after years of conditioning, I couldn't pee if I couldn't relax, and I couldn't relax if I couldn't sit. So with squatting essentially out of the picture, my experimentation was narrowed to various approaches to sitting. In my first attempts, I sat on low rocks. This led again to the puddle-up and splatter effect, the only difference being wet thighs instead of wet ankles.

Then came several tries directly on the ground, based on some left-over-from-college-physics notion that proximity decreases velocity, like pouring lemonade into a pie pan. Direct contact with the earth gave me a primordial closeness to nature but proved disastrous. Either I ended up seated in the puddle, or, trying a slight incline to avoid that, I wound up with a problem rather like trying to anticipate the flow of Kilauea's lava. How far and in which direction was that steaming stuff going to travel? Usually far enough to wipe out the jeans draped around my feet. Furthermore, leaves, burrs, twigs, and foxtails – all having a tendency to stick to my buns – would lodge themselves in my undergarments, ending up in more critical crannies.

A few more days of trial and error dampened yet another theory; sitting on higher objects merely encouraged a more direct route into the boots. But I remained undaunted, enjoying my freedom from walls too much to scurry back to a finely polished, containerized seat, and I set off in search of smoother surfaces away from the spray.

And here it is. For those of us whose squatting muscles have atrophied (a mutation that I'm certain paralleled the advent of privy seats), for those of us who didn't grow up on the farm or going fishing with grandpa, and for those of us who wish to experience a piss in the woods with the same high quality of enjoyment one experiences in devouring a piece of good New York cheesecake, here is the secret to not peeing in your boots.

First, leave camp in plenty of time to locate an inspiring view, far enough into the bush that your urethra won't tie itself into a bowline at the thought of "being seen." Remember: The *can* – the only mental relief available on occasion – acquires its reputation for offering restful respite largely because of its isolation. Now look for a spot with two rocks, or two logs, or a rock and a log close together. Slide your pants down around your ankles and seat yourself near the front edge of one rock. Then prop up your feet – off the ground – on the other. Here you can sit, relax, avoid all showers, and keep sticker free. The steep incline of a hillside, the side of a boulder, or a tree trunk can also be used as the second rock. If you're something of a rock climber, you can actually brace yourself in a narrow passageway between two flat-faced boulders or rock walls (a chimney, climbers call it) with your back flat against one side, your knees slightly bent, and your feet flat against the other. In the desert where there are no rocks and logs, you can still sit instead of squat to pee, on the edge of your pack or bedroll. In sandy soil there will be no splatters.

What's more, if you want to coolly flaunt – "this is no sweat for an old hand like me, I was born a frontierswoman" – find a two-rock spot behind a boulder or bush (waist high) from where you can casually, and with dignity intact, carry on a conversation with the rest of camp. Well, maybe not completely intact on the initial try. But be patient. The combination of *women*, *peeing*, and *dignity*, takes a bit of getting used to – not only for you, but for the people with whom you'll be conversing. Be brave. Act "as if" at first; appear nonchalant. Practice. Teach. Be persistent. Eventually the world will change. And in the meantime, keep your feet *up* and dry while gazing blissfully off over the misty mountaintops in complete peace and satisfaction.

◆

The other imperative for women traipsing around in the great outdoors is to develop a discreet, environmental approach to menstruation. You may never feel as brazen as one woman packer I observed stooped over a campfire and cooking breakfast for twenty people. Behind her ear, tucked into her sun-blond curls where one might stick a pencil, she sported a paper-clad tampon, just waiting for a moment's break in the chores. For most of us twentieth-century urban women of propriety traveling in the company of others (and also for any of us who'd rather not offer anyone opportunity to attribute our natural assertiveness to being "on the rag"), here is the plan.

First find a container in which to store your major monthly supply. I've used a regular tin bandage box or a lovely antique tin. This size works well for applicatorless tampons. A month's supply fits neatly into the small tin, and the tin snugly into the corner of an ammo can, lashed to a raft. When I'm driving horses and my hands stay dirty all day on the trail, I use tampons with applicators. These require a larger container. If you use sanitary pads, you will need one even roomier. The latest designer bag you brought home from boutique shopping, a soft satin travel case, or a plain plastic bag all work equally well. This main supply remains stowed away in the depths of your duffel bag or backpack.

Now you need a container for daily use – something to keep handy and slip into your pocket when you stroll off in search of your place of easement. A small cosmetic bag would work, though an ordinary ziplock bag will do. Inside you will keep a day's supply of whatever you're using as well as several other small plastic bags and a cache of toilet paper or a pocket packet of tissue. The latter is a good choice since tissues can be handed out quite politely to others in need and also tucked into a pocket if your day kit becomes too jammed with refuse by the end of the day. You'll use the additional plastic bags to store inorganic refuse – t.p., used tampons and sanitary pads, and any paper or cellophane wrappers – which *must* be packed out. For the rest of the day, the refuse bags will reside inside your day kit, which can be stashed in your pocket, a fanny pack, a saddle bag, an ammo can, or an outside pocket of a backpack.

At evening camp when you resupply your day kit, you can transfer the refuse bags to the your main supply bag. Or you might add them to the central group garbage container, should there be one.

On organized expeditions the garbage is sorted into burnable and pack-out refuse. To limit the volume and weight of the pack-out garbage, the paper trash is burned in the evening fire or the last thing before breaking camp. Keep in mind that tampons and sanitary napkins need a hot fire to be completely consumed. Once a long time ago, when I was a novice in my newly acquired environmental awareness, I returned to camp under cover of darkness and surreptitiously slipped a small carefully wadded bundle into the coals. While we drank Swiss Miss, sang songs, and exchanged flip and wrap stories, to my horror the fire slowly blackened and curled away only the wrappings of my gift. The safest thing to do on a group trip is ask the leader or one of the guides about disposal procedures.

Finally, be aware that plastic when burned puts deadly poison into the air. Therefore, when you dump stuff into the burnable trash, keep your plastic bag for the pack-out garbage.

◆

A word here on feminine funnels: These devices to facilitate a woman's peeing are obtainable in washable, reusable plastic or disposable paper and should by rights be available in every public toilet. There are several designs, some accompanied by various lengths of hose. The principle is the same for all models: The funnel, elongated and elliptical in shape, affords a comfortable fit between a woman's legs and allows her to direct her stream.

Funnels have been used successfully in convalescent hospitals and by women in wheelchairs. I first saw them advertised in *Latitude 38*, a marine publication. They were delighting women sailors who could use them to avoid going below in order to *go* – a ship's cramped head being the worst spot to hang out if you're prone to seasickness. The funnel entailed no dropping of drawers – only an unzipping of shorts or pulling aside of a bathing suit. Women could stand tall, hip to hip, with the men, and pee over the rail.

My initial excitement about funnels was in the thought that they might be precisely the solution for sleeping out on nippy nights. With a hose, I might pee at 4:00 A.M. without having to crawl out of my toasty bag. Upon first use one disadvantage became immediately apparent. The longest of the coiled hoses (and you need the longest in this situation) has a strong memory. With persistence you can stretch it out, but let go and the end flops around to spray everything in sight like an out of control fire hose. In addition, if you expect the liquid to exit the correct end, you must remember the principle of gravity. Having gone to the trouble of hunting up a perfectly flat spot on which to bed, you will have to work hard to stay wrapped in the warmth of your bedroll while raising yourself enough to provide a downhill flow. Though I hear reports from women who manage this well, I say forget it! A few moments of scampering about in the frost makes you all the more appreciative of a warm bag – part of the daily allotment of minor inconveniences and miseries that help us retain a healthy perspective on life. Finally, if you're inside a tent and rain or sleet is pelting the sides, the old coffee can works fine.

Funnels, as I see it, are most serviceable in public toilets, adding a convenient frontal attack to grandmother's stand-up peeing style. One woman I know has carried hers all over Europe; now she's never without it.

For anyone interested in experimenting with a funnel, the investment will be small. I've reprinted the names and addresses of two companies that manufacture funnels, because to locate them on hearsay requires the assistance of a well trained librarian.

Freshette, both plastic and heavy paper models, varied lengths
   of hose, and collector bags
   Sani-fem Corporation
   7415 Stewart & Gray Road, Downey, CA 90241
   (213) 928-3435

Le Funnelle, lightweight paper with a handle, each packaged
   with a snip of t.p., advertised for "when you are on the
   town, out of town, cannot sit down..."
   Aplex Corporation
   1720 S. Amphlett Blvd., Suite 217, San Mateo, CA 94402
   (415) 341-8198

In closing this chapter and to warm your hearts, I
pass along the following funnel story related to me by
an employee of a Sausalito yachting supply house:

> After carefully selecting a pink plastic funnel, an
> elderly, white-haired couple arrived at the cash regis-
> ter, whereupon the woman sweetly inquired whether
> a longer hose might be attached for her. Her request
> was gladly granted and the funnel whisked away to
> the back workroom. Then, lifting her gentle, wisdom-
> aged face toward her husband, with a cherubic wink
> she crooned, "Now, dear, mine will be longer than
> yours!"

WHAT? NO T.P.? OR DOING WITHOUT

Back to the Pleistocene

An *Earth First* bumpersticker

Conjure up for a moment one of those predawn suburban mornings when you emerge reluctantly from the warm bedding and randomly bump along the walls to the bathroom to sit, just another shadow hunched on the bowl. With eyes shut against the real world, elbows deeply dug into your knees and chin hidden in a cradle of knuckles, you are soon drowsily appreciating the serenity following a particularly portly poop. Then, wishing you could transport yourself back to horizontal and disappear into nothingness again, you blindly grope for the toilet paper only to find that your fingertips are spinning a naked cylinder of cardboard with the flapping racket of a pinwheel. Rats! You're forced to flip on one hundred watts, stumble across the room to the cabinet under the sink, and fish out and unwrap a new roll. You might exchange it for the empty one (if you were really a good person), but the dexterity involved would require your final emergence from dreamland.

Or how about one of those ghastly dinner parties that are not casual and not just old friends? It could be a Waterford and Limoges setting at the elderly boss's estate or maybe a new girlfriend's esteemed literary family gathered to look you over. The seven-course meal has been consumed, yet the intercourse has not relaxed. As a matter of fact, the guests are perched around the ornate living room like so many stately and stoic great blue herons, picking quietly at thin-layered desserts and sipping tea. Quite suddenly amidst all this propriety, the spiced prune conserve (which had accompanied the main course and is now somewhere south of your stomach) screams at you to leap up and excuse yourself – politely, of course – on the pretense of helping (the maid?) with the dishes.

Once into the hallway, with pointed toes lifted high in double time, you detour to the bathroom in a perfect imitation of Sylvester the Cat. Shortly thereafter comes the discovery that your hostess has neglected to renew the supply of toilet paper, which – unbeknownst to you – she keeps in the hall closet. You've finished crawling through all the cupboards: Now what? Do you hobble to the door with your pants around your knees, poke your nose through the crack, and coolly call, "psst!"? When people disappear into the bathroom at a party, everyone imagines them peering into the mirror checking for spinach between their teeth, "freshening-up," or, possibly tinkling. Straining and pooping? Never. All pretenses go out the window when you holler for toilet paper (in a pinch, women will drip-dry for Number One just like men). For the rest of the evening you may as well wear a sandwich board with three-foot headlines proclaiming what you've been up to.

For pure perspective, I recount these or equally painful paperless scenarios when people respond to the thought of experimenting in the woods without toilet paper as if they'd just fallen into a vat of putrefying fish guts! There's nothing so disgusting about it, really.

As with all major changes, adjusting to the absence of that readily available soft and quilted white stuff wound neatly around a cylinder takes a bit of getting used to. Though once successfully maneuvered, brushing one's posterior with a snatch of biodegradable nature can provide a noteworthy experience whereupon one's ecologically proscribed place in the universe may come vividly into focus. Or even puffed up with ecological pride or jubilant with primitive freedom, one might be startled to hear a rousing chorus of approval from the forest fairies. So I've been told.

Doing without t.p. takes me back – way back. Mr. Neanderthal might have had skin like horsehide and needn't have bothered with wiping; but I swear I can sense him and his buddies in their ghostly forms lurking about, curious every time I walk away from a purely organic burial of shit and leaves. After an accomplishment of this sort, I bounce jauntily along absurdly pleased with myself, a euphoric little note within a great harmony. Such mysterious brushes with my deepest origins not only overwhelm but refresh me, as tangibly as a hot shower after a week of mountain sweat and dirt. All at once I feel powerfully attached to a cosmic whole, simple in an age of complexity, perfectly in tune yet tiny and humble, and, of all things, enchantingly ancient. Vats of putrefying fish guts – phooey!

Be it a personal quest to function as simply as the primeval wandering tribes, or the thought of not having to pack around rolls of bulky tissue and bags of carry-out garbage – whatever your motivation, a few suggestions follow to get you started. The library is not full of pertinent references to t.p. alternatives, and I will never have covered enough ground to have all the answers. You will have to depart from the text after finishing this chapter and experiment on your own. Call it scientific research.

When I began my evaluation of leaves, I remembered a dear high school friend who had traveled across Europe keeping a toilet paper dairy, complete with sample bits from different countries. She returned to the States with everything from pieces of brown wrapping paper to wax paper and Saran Wrap. Is it, I wonder, worth speculating on the regional correlations between indigenous plant leaves and present day toilet paper quality? If you think you have trouble selecting brands in the supermarket, wait until you see the spectrum nature has to offer.

A vast assortment of leaves, some obviously more appropriate to the task than others, are yours for the picking. But wait. A few critical words of caution are necessary first:

> *There are many items suitable for substitute toilet paper, and the choice of living plants should only be a last resort. If you pick leaves at all, be especially mindful. Always select dead grasses and leaves over live ones. Don't pick wildflowers or rare species. Don't pick in parks or other restricted areas. Don't pull anything up by the roots. Don't rob large clumps or strip an entire branch. Carefully pick a leaf here, a leaf there – so no one, not even the plant (especially the plant), will know that you have been there. In the following pages you will find many suggestions for nonliving t.p. substitutes.*

To hunt leaves, an introductory course in botany is unnecessary; nor must you learn every leaf by name. But engrave in your memory photographs of poison oak, ivy, sumac, and those nasty stinging nettles, illustrated in any good field guide. A dinner date with Frankenstein's monster or the Wicked Witch of the West would be a joyous interlude compared to the aftermath of using these on your keister. If you're hanging around Neanderthaloid apparitions and you're also a member of the New Age species I call Exotic Trekkies (those who roam about in exotic climates), I recommend you read up on the vegetation indigenous to the regions you plan to visit to ascertain whether some peculiar variety of viperous honeysuckle or poison pine ought to be included in your don't-touch list.

Whenever leafstalking, look for the large and the soft. Mullein leaves are my favorite: soft, cushy, almost woolly, and usually one leaf will do. Plants with small or palmated leaves can be used by the handful (remember – one here, one there). Frequently there will be no perfect specimen available. At those times, the profusion and ample diameters of leaves such as California's wild grape may offer compensation for their wax paper slickness.

Before picking be sure to examine leaves carefully; they can sometimes be sticky (as though covered by a thin layer of syrup), scabrous (having a rasp-like surface), annoyingly prickly owing to small bristles and barbs, or, more seriously, hispidulous (covered with sharp hairs stiff enough to penetrate the skin). Stay away from reeds, bamboo, and some grasses – in effect, slicing leaves – that can cause agonizing wounds like paper cuts. With a little care you'll learn which ones to avoid and be on your way to becoming a connoisseur of fine leaves.

Autumn woodlands – not to be shamed by the swankiest powder room decor – offer us a leaf selection in vibrant designer shades. Not all fallen leaves dry and crumble immediately. Many will stay pliable through the winter months. Alpine winters, where deciduous vegetation is scarce, can be a bit of a problem. For a matter of months in many parts of the high country, evergreens are virtually the only selection. With a little creativity, you can put pine needles to good use, provided you have the time to line them all up in the same direction. Sticks can be useful if you remember to rub *with* the grain. Pine cones are also reputedly good tools. Steer clear of the spiny rotund cones and stick with the narrower, softer, older sorts. A world-renowned river rafter I know swears by old spongy Douglas fir cones.

My cross-country skiing partner promotes snowballs as the perfect winter wipe – that is, once you've braced yourself for the momentary shock. Try it. To me the freeze is a minor trauma compared to a visit to one of those portable plastic chemical toilets that sit on construction sites or in many campgrounds, exuding breathtaking aromas from the contents cooking within.

Let's return to the glorious woods. In your rummagings around in the great outdoors for t.p.-like items, you're bound to find many suitable materials. Try sheets of smooth peeling bark, polished driftwood, seashells, and large feathers. Steer clear of mosses; they're fragile, shouldn't be disturbed, and crumble uselessly anyway.

In the rural areas of many countries, there are people who have never laid eyes on toilet paper. In parts of the Middle East, a person carries a wet cloth into the fields. The custom of eating religiously with only the right hand was not born of divine Arab vision but of prudent hygiene; the left hand wiped. I wouldn't want to discourage you if this particular technique works for you, but before settling on it permanently, you might consider that for environmental reasons (covered in

Chapter Two) this method will entail carrying along a cloth and two small buckets for rinsing. The second bucket is used to rinse out the first so as to avoid dipping the fecally contaminated wash bucket directly into the water. Afterwards all wash and rinse water must be buried well away from any watercourse.

Arid, sandy terrains are the most critically lacking in t.p. substitutes. In a dry creek bed you can sometimes find a smooth sun-baked stone – state of the art in wipe! But caution is required. Under a blazing sun, stones can gather enough heat to brand cattle! Before using a stone, test it in your hand and on your wrist as you would a baby bottle. And remember not to redeposit a used stone in the creek bed.

There you have it: All I know today. Now you're on your own.

Hmm. Well, I once met a man who suggested using sand on my bum in the mountain man's age-old manner of scouring pots and pans. But I have a hunch this curmudgeonly old bugger was, or had, like my own Mr. N., a horsehide's ass! I think I'll stick to snowballs and stones.

Definition of Shit

¹**shit** /'shit/*vb*. **shit** *or* **shat** \'shat\; **shit-ting** [alter. (influenced by ²shit and the past and pp. forms) of earlier *shite*, fr. ME *shiten*, fr. OE *-scitan*; akin to MLG & MD *schiten* to defecate, OHG *scizan*, ON *skita* to defecate, OE *sceadan* to divide or separate – more at SHED] *v.i.* 1. to defecate; often used figuratively to express embarrassment <I thought I'd ~ when I had to pee and there wasn't any place to hide.> or fear <I just about ~ when I stepped off the ski lift and viewed the hill from above.>. ~ *v.t.* to defecate something <~ watery stools>. 2. to fool, to mislead, to put on <You wouldn't ~ me about using pine cones for toilet paper, would you?>

shit can; 1. to throw away. 2. to ban. 3. to fire.

shit fruit salad (also: shit nickels, shit ice cream); said of a prima donna <she's so special, she must ~>.

shit on; 1. to ruin, to muck up. 2. to treat unfairly, often by being extremely rude or unkind or harsh.

shit the bed; to foul your nest; to stupidly mess up your own good situation.

²**shit** \'shit\ *n*. [fr. (assumed) ME, fr. OE *scite* (attested only in place names); akin to MD *schit, schitte* excrement, OE *scitan* to defecate] 1. a: feces b: garbage; junk; unorganized or unrelated articles, stuff <Never leave ~ in the woods>. 2. lies, nonsense, exaggeration <a bunch of ~>.

bad shit; a consumable of piss-poor quality; generally refers to street drugs.

big shit; someone with an overinflated sense of self-importance.

blow (a person's) shit away; to kill; figuratively, to astound.

built like a brick shit house; well built.

bullshit; 1. lies; nonsense. 2. trash; useless junk. 3. name of a group word game. 4. an interjection of fierce disagreement.

can eat sawdust and shit 2x4's; is overworked.

chickenshit; 1. *n*. a coward. 2. *adj*. cowardly.

crock of shit; something false or deceptive <campaign promises are usually a ~>.

deep shit; big trouble; also stated *knee deep in shit*.

dipshit; idiot.

dish out shit; to deliver reprimands or punishments; also, to abuse verbally.

do bears shit in the woods?; rhetorical reply to statement of the obvious.

doesn't know shit from Shinola; can't tell the difference between excrement and brown shoe polish.

dogshit; 1. low-down, dirty, trashed-out. 2. interjection expressing hot disapproval.

don't give me that shit; same as "Seems to me I've heard that song before."

dumbshit; a pathetic incompetent.

eat shit, 1. to lose a game by a large margin. 2. to get a very raw deal; to absorb or withstand many insults or even physical abuse. 3. to humble oneself. 4. an angry demand, meaning to go away, to drop dead.

get your shit together; 1. undergo great personal growth; become organized or focused. 2. admonition to hurry up.

give a shit; to care <Mother Nature dear, we do ~>.

good shit; a product of excellent quality; flavorful; generally a reference to street drugs.

Holy shit!; exclamation of surprise, discovery, realization, or fear.

horseshit; 1. lies; double-talk. 2. interjection of vehement disagreement.

hot shit; a class act; a popular item; frequently used sarcastically <just because he climbed Everest, he thinks he's ~>.

jack shit; a negative value; to do *jack shit* is to do less than nothing.

know your shit; to be an expert in your field.

little shit; 1. person of small stature. 2. petty annoyance. 3. term of endearment for one who is looked upon almost admiringly as a sweet rascal.

No shit!; 1. exclamation expressing excitement and surprise; similar to *Really?*; may be used sarcastically in response to something already known. 2. an exclamation of hearty agreement.

Oh shit!; exclamation of surprise or disgust; when pronounced \oo shit\ generally a warning of impending doom; can also mean merely *Whoops!*; when pronounced \o shee'it\ indicates great pain or embarrassment, or a colossal disaster; when pronounced \aw shit\ expresses regret or sympathy.

old shit; things or ideas which have become outmoded; behavior patterns that no longer work; old baggage or agendas.

piece of shit; 1. cheaply constructed article 2. bad person.

scare the living shit out of; terrorize.

shit-end of the stick; the rotten part of a deal.

a shit; a derogatory term.

shit happens; expresses the sentiment "the best laid plans often go awry"; often seen on bumper stickers.

shit hits the fan; 1. a violent or unpleasant situation, often in reference to reprimands coming down from authority figures. 2. a major organizational shake-up.

Shit, man! /'shēt män/ 1. generic exclamation for surprise, disgust, delight, anger. 2. expression of pleasure, appreciation, astonishment.

shit on a brick; a rude exclamation expressing great disgust.

shit on a shingle; creamed chipped beef on toast.

shit on wheels; 1. someone who gets a lot done. 2. a holy terror. 3. a braggart who nevertheless carries it off.

shit or get off the pot; quit wasting time or stalling.

shit out of luck; having ill fortune.

shitcan; toilet; garbage can; honey bucket.

the shits; 1. diarrhea. 2. a dreary, rotten situation; <camping in this cold, damp cave full of bats is ~>.

stay out of my shit; admonition to mind your own business, to stop meddling.

sure as shit; a very definite and sometimes predictable occurrence; true to form.

take a shit; to defecate.

take shit; to accept abuse or ridicule.

tough shit; 1. expression indicating bad luck, similar to *Too bad!* or *That's the way the cookie crumbles!* 2. *angry response to a person's excuses, stronger than So what!*

up shit creek; in a bad situation.

shit-ass *n*. a reprehensible individual.

shit-bird *n*. a mild, sometimes half affectionate name for a scoundrel.

shit-brain *n*. an idiot.

shit disturber *n*. an instigator.

shit faced *adj*. drunk or otherwise intoxicated.

shit-fire *n*. a mean, nasty person; a bully.

shit-fit *n*. a temper tantrum; a tizzy.

shit-head *n*. halfway between a *shit-ass* and a *shit-bird*.

shit hole *n*. 1. a. a toilet b. the hole in the privy board; often used figuratively <Financing the research for a biodegradable bag for packing it out would not be throwing money down the ~>. 2. the anus.

shit house *n*. 1. a bathroom or outhouse.
in the shit house; in disrepute.
shit house poet; 1. anyone who scribbles graffiti on restroom walls. 2. a lousy poet.

shit list *n*. figurative list, implies persons held in low esteem <the person who forgot to pack the toilet paper is on everyone's ~>.

shit load *n*. big, huge, behemoth.

shit shark *n*. the person who operates the honey wagon.

shitter *n*. an outhouse; a toilet.
in the shitter; in disrepute.
shitter time; a place to think things out; discipline in a drug rehab program.

shitty /shit-ē/ *adj.*, **shit-ti-er**; **-est** 1. inept. 2. inferior, cheap, bad, or ugly; denotes a state of being that is somehow dreadful, often as a result of physical pain or guilt <I peed right down that little mole's hole and now I feel ~>.

Afterword

We need to foster a bosom friendship with land and water and air. I did not once write the word *wilderness* in these pages without some cringing and self-evaluation; I remember the telling words of Chief Luther Standing Bear of the Oglala Sioux:

> We did not think of the great open plains, the beautiful rolling hills, and winding streams with tangled growth, as "wild." Only to the white man was nature a "wilderness" and only to him was the land "infested" with "wild" animals and "savage" people. To us it was tame. Earth was bountiful and we were surrounded with the blessings of the Great Mystery. Not until the hairy man from the east came and with brutal frenzy heaped injustices upon us and the families we loved was it "wild" for us. When the very animals of the forest began fleeing from his approach, then it was that for us the "Wild West" began.